F.R.E.E.D.O.M.

F.R.E.E.D.O.M.

Essays on America's Fight for Freedom

James Liberty

iUniverse, Inc.

Bloomington

F.R.E.E.D.O.M.
Essays on America's Fight for Freedom

iUniverse books may be ordered through booksellers or by contacting:

iUniverse
1663 Liberty Drive
Bloomington, IN 47403
www.iuniverse.com
1-800-Authors (1-800-288-4677)

Because of the dynamic nature of the Internet, any web addresses or links contained in this book may have changed since publication and may no longer be valid. The views expressed in this work are solely those of the author and do not necessarily reflect the views of the publisher, and the publisher hereby disclaims any responsibility for them.

Any people depicted in stock imagery provided by Thinkstock are models, and such images are being used for illustrative purposes only.

Certain stock imagery © Thinkstock.

ISBN: 978-1-4759-3765-7 (sc)
ISBN: 978-1-4759-3767-1 (hc)
ISBN: 978-1-4759-3766-4 (e)

Library of Congress Control Number: 2012914311

Printed in the United States of America

iUniverse rev. date: 09/17/2012

This book is dedicated to the people I love most in my life:

To my wife and best friend Amy, who is so beautiful inside and out. Love you!

Mom – maybe my biggest fan, along with dad. I love you so much. The best mom ever!

Dad –my best man! I would not be able to do so many things in life without you. You are the man!

Duke – the best dog a boy could ever have.

Peanut – the most loyal dog on the planet, to Amy.

Becks, Bill, Meredith, Ryan, Jake, Lisa and Billy, cousins and friends.

Anthony De Mello- who although died 25 years ago, taught me so many life changing lesson through his books and videos. I'll forever be grateful. Here are just a few of them:

A.) "Life is easy, life is delightful. It's only hard on your illusions, your ambitions, your greed, and your cravings."
B.) "We are all born with happiness. You don't acquire it, you already have it. Then why don't you experience it? Drop the illusion, your attachments and all that remains is happiness"
C.) "Peacefully content always> only the content are truly free!"

Contents

Foreword

Before we touch upon the seven most important subjects for freedom in our lifetime, I want to reflect on just how fortunate we are to be living on this great planet. This will allow for some debt of gratitude and perspective before tackling these complex subjects.

By the grace of God we are here: According to widely acclaimed authors Gonzalez and Richards of *The Privileged Planet*, Earth is within the galactic habitable zone, orbiting a main sequence g2 dwarf star, protected by giant planets, within a circumsteller habitable zone, a nearly circular orbit, an oxygen rich atmosphere, the correct mass, orbited by 1 large moon, a magnetic field, plate tectonics, correct ratio of liquid water, continents, a terrestrial planet, moderate rate of rotation and more...there are around 20 main factors that have allowed earth to be the most hospitable place for humans to live. If we give each of those factors a very, very conservative 1/10 chance of them all happening at the same time, we are left with a figure of: 1/1,000,000,000,000,000. So with 1/10 chance of all 20 factors happening at the same time to the same planet, we are left with a one in one thousandth of a trillion chance of our planet coming together just the way it has...consider yourself very lucky. Remember those 20 factors were only given a 1/10 chance, imagine what the number would be if each were given a 1 in a million chance! I have asked for contemplation on these amazing figures because I don't feel like people truly appreciate how fortunate we are to be here. Knowledge is power and remembering how privileged we are helps us to enjoy the time we have. The complexity of all these events happening in just the right way, to just our planet is mind-boggling. On top of which, we've come to find that Earth was setup precisely for the discovery and understandings of how our planet works. Earth was designed for life to flourish. In summary, the complexity of it all makes you realize that some greater force is at work. God had to be responsible for the unbelievable planet that he gave to us. We should all be so very grateful to him for making life possible.

Introduction

F.R.E.E.D.O.M is an acronym for the most essential issues in American politics today. These seven topics provide remarkable insight as to how and why America's freedom is being threatened by enemies inside and outside of this great nation. F.R.E.E.D.O.M clearly communicates which radical terrorists groups wish to do us harm, what they are doing to accomplish their acts of terror and who is helping them from within our borders. It outlines how our healthcare is radically changing to socialized medicine and what we can do to stop it. F.R.E.E.D.O.M shows the difference between socialist countries versus those that embrace capitalism. It also illustrates how driving our debt ceiling to disastrous heights, is slowly but surely enslaving the American people. Next, we examine America's ever-evolving energy situation and reveal who continues to prevent America from extracting our own natural resources. After that we dig deep into the chaos of climate change to discover who is setting the agenda and what role it plays in our energy supply. F.R.E.E.D.O.M then seeks to obtain a greater understanding of America's education system and the socialized propaganda that has infiltrated our school system. Finally, we take a look at the misinformation spewed from the mainstream media in order to influence and control our decisions at the behest of big government liberalism.

The purpose of this book is to provide clarity and understanding to make educated decisions to maintain your freedom. My hope is that the guideline put forth by F.R.E.E.D.O.M can be instrumental in your decision making process when voting in the 2012 election. You will discover the difference between clarity and emotion and truth over mob mentality when comparing conservative and liberal ideals. F.R.E.E.D.O.M will enable you to rise above the misinformation purposely put out by the mainstream media and alert you to the coercive nature of big government liberalism. Liberals in this country, combined with the backing of our state controlled media, are tearing apart the fundamental ideas with which this country was founded upon. Liberal leaders seek a society void of pliableness. Yes, they may say they want change, but what they really want is power. When liberal leaders grab hold of this power they use it to continually strive for order, orthodoxy, routine and conformity. Or put another way – they want you the individual, dumb and numb. Dumb, so they may pass laws and shape society to control the masses. Numb, so that when you are told over and over again that government is the cure, the individual becomes numb to the repetitive message that life without government rule would not be possible. It is this sad and coercive message that has flowed from liberal leaders throughout history and has now infiltrated close to 40% of America. This in turn, has pushed our once beautiful country down the path of socialism. Yet, we must not let America slide into an apathetic way of life, like Europe or South America by falling into the trap of big government. Only by wrestling freedom back from the jaws of big government rule can America regain its place as the greatest nation on earth, as freedom will return to the rightful hands of the individual.

My Journey

It is imperative that you know how this book became a reality. My interest in politics began shortly after 9/11. Then again that would not be entirely fair because I was still in college and everybody knows that when you are in college you are not really dialed in to what is happening around the country. You are consumed with having fun, meeting members of the opposite sex and being a student. More accurately my interests began in

2005. My path towards political curiosity began like this: I woke up in a room not knowing where I was or what had happened. I had no idea a helicopter had just life-flighted me to a hospital somewhere in the Midwest. As time passed, I could occasionally hear the rhythmic sound of beep…beep…beep on the respirator as I slipped in and out of consciousness. It was a comforting sound because I could revel in the fact that I was alive. Those beeps signaled to me that oxygen continued to flow into my battered body. At times, I heard distant voices pouring out heartfelt words of encouragement like, "we are with you" and "I love you" as my mother and father stood by my side. During the two quiet days I spent in the hospital room there were IV's, needles and tubes to keep me company. I even had a catheter that a nurse stepped on causing great pain in the area "down below." The "accident" had left me with a near fracture to the back of my skull, blurred vision, a broken nose, fractured cheekbone, broken orbital bones, a deeply lacerated chin and general soreness throughout my body. I had no idea at the time but my journey into politics began then and there in that hospital room. A transformation had taken place but not in the "all at once" type of transformation that takes place in the movies. It was a gradual and somewhat painful process. Although I was always aware of the dangers one faces, the "accident" had left a clear reminder of just how precious life can be. I became more serious, more reclusive, more scared but more thoughtful. Months slowly passed by as I was stuck at home with bad vision, unable to see up or down because the orbital bones were shattered around my eyes. The reduction in eyesight left me with very few options. I could sit there wasting away, squinting at the television, watching nothing of importance or I could start reading about topics that had always interested me. I began reading about politics. I always had a vague interest in politics, but with three or four months with nothing to do, my curiosity spiked to a whole new level. I read and read and read some more…

After my injuries healed, I began working at my father's insurance company. I was living with my parents and had a 35 min drive to work everyday. I quickly became bored with the standard commute and needed much more than just music to get me through my morning drive. My dad suggested I try political talk radio. It was a logical suggestion since the past four months had already wetted my appetite. I swiftly replied, "Thanks, but no thanks." How could I sit there listening to the sound of other people talking instead of energetic songs? Well, this was turning point number two in my road to politics. I began to realize just how much farther I needed to go in order to fully grasp the issues we Americans face today. Before long, the large amount of contradictory statements between radio and television began to pile up. I found it hard to decipher between the talking heads on television that sent one message, while those on the radio and internet sent a completely different signal. I needed to find more than just memorized congressional maneuvering, I needed answers! I wanted to get to the root of our political issues to figure out why some people believe socialism is great and others believe in capitalism. Why do some people insist on believing in global warming while others know that our climate changes naturally? Why do some say we should continue enhanced interrogation while others say we should have no part in kill/capture programs? Why haven't we faced that fact radical Islam has a problem with us? Is drilling for our own natural resources really causing lasting damage to our planet? These and other questions began to slowly but surely call to me and I had to find the truth. At first it was an anxiety producing experience. I wanted to know the correct answer to every issue, immediately! As everyone knows, it takes time and patience. I eventually decided that I needed to give the radio gurus a try. At first my attention span was painfully short as I found it unbearable listening to intense political banter, especially in the morning. However, I kept at it and forced myself to really pay attention to arguments on both sides of the aisle. As fall turned into winter and winter became spring my political interests were at an all- time high. Yet, I realized that I still needed to enhance my knowledge base by leaps and bounds and the only way to do that was to get organized.

I needed some way to categorize the main political topics because there are so many points to study. Eventually, I came up with an acronym to frame the most important issues in American politics. That acronym became: F.R.E.E.D.O.M. It is challenging to understand all the issues facing our nation. Try asking one of our congressmen about climate change and you'll be hard pressed to find anything close to an intelligent response.

A politician's ability to circumvent the issue is called answering a question without really saying anything at all! I came to the conclusion that I had to spread the word. The truth was out there, but substantive answers were chaotic at best. I have spent the last five years trying to get the correct ones, and it wasn't easy. When I turned on the television, I would think to myself...did he or she really say anything? Usually the answer was no. Well the aggravation ends here. Through painstaking research, time, energy, curiosity, patience, frustration and success I hope to provide insight into the most pressing political points of our time. After reading this book it is my hope that people will for the first time really understand the basis for these political issues and choose a side based on reasoning and facts rather than talking points and misinformation.

F is for "Fighting" Terrorists

The crusades have evolved from knights on horseback fighting in hand-to-hand combat against Persian warriors to modern day jihadist using infiltration as their weapon of choice. No longer is the level of one's swordsmanship of any importance, nor the size of one's army. One thousand years ago, the crusaders could readily see the enemy advancing towards them, in which a battle to the death was inevitable. In today's age, the greatest asset of the modern day fighter is the ability to avoid detection behind enemy lines, not confront his sworn enemy with an invading army. Terrorists surreptitiously move about our own country, plotting and planning right under our noses. Yet, in today's fight for freedom, we find one element remarkably different. Terrorists now operate with two advantages: appeasement and political correctness. These two corrosive concepts are front and center of the liberal agenda and have come to be the defining characteristics of the left and are damaging America from the inside out. Liberal appeasement and political correctness are the name of the game these days. Even when it's painfully apparent that an act of terror was committed in the name of religion, the left refuses to acknowledge it. My friends, this is becoming a metaphorical noose around our neck that keeps getting tighter each day. The mission of today's radical Islamists is simple: penetrate our society, blend in, and adopt our fashion, our dialect, our jobs, and befriend us all in the name of jihad. If this were America's only problem it would be bad enough. However, America is not just battling radical Islam. We are up against an enemy that doesn't realize what it is doing. An enemy that has gone so far off the path of common sense that it can no longer see its way back to reality. Overzealous liberals that are too prideful to see past their own misguided notions of so-called compassion and fairness. Relentless appeasement has only emboldened each stealth jihad fighter as he gathers support not just from his homeland but our homeland as well. The ability to aptly defend this great nation is becoming harder and harder each day because of the liberal mentality that has seeped into society. To call a terrorist a terrorist seems, well… racist in the eyes of the left. We are seeing the walls of protection from enemies foreign and domestic begin to crumble and crack. These falling pieces are remnants of the constitution, the words of sound reasoning, now resembling mere shards of their former self.

Remember, radicals only need an army of one. One to hear the anti American message in his mosque, one to receive the toxic drivel of a Marxist revolutionary, one to believe the left wing propaganda and one to detonate a bomb. One is all it takes to perform the cowardice act of a suicide bomb resulting in the death of millions of innocent Americans. Political correctness cannot win the day. You do not protect American citizens by groping grandmas in the airport while in the same breath appeasing terrorists even when they are in the wrong. You don't call the Islamic gunman at Ford Hood an unhappy murderer. No, you call him what he is, nothing more, nothing less - an Islamic radical terrorist. He committed murder in the name of jihad, taking the lives of 13 innocent American soldiers and wounding 29 others. America cannot continue down the path of constructing mosque after mosque when 85% of Islamic leaders preach in American mosques in some form or another hatred of the United States, as reported (quietly) by the mainstream media. This appeasement must stop! Voices of reason based in reality must come forth. Common sense must shine light on the fact that waterboarding is a life saving technique and provides crucial information for future terrorist plots. Common sense must penetrate the liberal walls of incompetence to reveal why we must continue taking the fight to the enemy in Afghanistan rather than backpedal and retreat in hopes that the enemy will just give up. The fight against radicals remains an ever-present threat with dangerous enemies lurking not only abroad but within our borders as well. The salvation of the United States is in great peril and yet liberals continue to undermine America's efforts to protect this great nation by appeasing and aiding radical terrorists in their mission of jihad. Liberal appeasement is playing an extremely dangerous game with every one of our lives. The reason America has stayed safe since 9/11 is due entirely to the efforts of past conservative action despite the repeated efforts of liberals to handcuff our military and encourage the enemy. Common sense conservatives are America's only hope for protection against radicals determined to do us harm. It is time for Americans to finally grasp which side of America cares about protecting you and your family.

The attack on our soil

Remembering 9/11...do you remember the emotions that stirred in you when you saw American Airlines flight 11 and United Airlines flight 175 crash into the North and South Towers of lower Manhattan? It's difficult to imagine how intensely scared our fellow Americans must have been while trapped in those planes. The only thing they could do was watch as they raced toward destruction. All that remained was the smell of burnt fuel mixed with toxic dust filling lower Manhattan as victims struggled for air inside and out of those fallen towers. Some even resorted to free falling to their death rather than succumb to the flames inside. Can you recall the brave men and women of the New York fire and police departments running into those buildings, providing leadership and bravery while putting the lives others ahead of their own? Equally as heroic were the citizens of United Flight 93, who sacrificed their own lives by keeping Islamic terrorists from completing their mission of flying into the Capitol or White House. Please, never forget those murdered at the Pentagon and the innocent Americans stuck in American Airlines flight 77 as it flew into the side of America's national defense building. What a scary moment in

American history. It was the first time most of us thought we are at war on our own soil. In all honesty, nothing has been the same for me since 9/11 and unfortunately the threat of terrorism is a real possibility everyday. Ever since that day I've been seeking answers to where the terrorists came from, why they hate us and what is this fight all about.

Who are they and where did they come from? Main problems: Hezbollah, Iran, Saudi Arabia, Al-Queda, Taliban

Terrorism against the United States began well before 9/11. In 1983 the terrorist attacks in Beirut killed 241 Marines, at the hands of radical Islamists. That was the single deadliest day for the Marine Core since Iwo Jima of World War II. In 1993 Islamic terrorists tried to blow up our Twin Towers using a truck bomb. Although the main goal was unsuccessful they did manage to kill 6 people and injured over 1,000 people. In 1996, truck bombs exploded at the embassy in Saudi Arabia, the product of radical Islamists. Some say this horrendous act was the work of Hezbollah while others believe it was Al-Queda. Regardless of which group it was, radical Islam was responsible for murdering 19 US Air Force airmen. Then in 1998, Islamic terrorists bombed the United States embassies in Tanzania and Kenya, killing 224 innocent souls in Nairobi and injuring over 5,000. In Kenya they succeeded in murdering 11 innocent people and injuring around 86 more. These atrocious acts were done together as 2 simultaneous truck bomb explosions were set off in an attempt to target American workers. In the year 2000, the USS Cole was attacked by radical terrorists who sent a suicide boat charging into the side of our Naval destroyer causing a 40 x 40 gash and resulting in the death of 17 sailors. The radicals also managed to injure 39 US sailors, making it the deadliest attack on a United States naval vessel since the Iraqi attack on the USS Stark in 1987. Can we see a pattern here? Every single one of those egregious attacks were planned and executed by radical Islam who specifically targeted American workers or serviceman in the name of jihad.

This brings us to Hezbollah

Hezbollah, a terrorist network formed in Iran, is the most extensive terrorist group in the world. They operate in over 40 countries on five continents with operations along the U.S. – Mexico border. Hezbollah has put major emphasis on gaining strength in Latin America, specifically Argentina, Brazil and Paraguay. Brazil has become this terrorist organizations biggest hub in order to trade cocaine for weapons with Colombia. Hezbollah has been a thorn in the side of both the United States and Israel's defense departments since the early 1980s. Before 9/11, you could say that Hezbollah was responsible for more American deaths than any other group. Besides Iran, Hezbollah enjoys close relations with both Syria and Venezuela through dictator Hugo Chavez. Yet, the biggest problem with Hezbollah is that they have operations in at least 15 U.S. cities! Their main purpose is to position themselves in different locations to obtain better launching points for a combined attack with Iran on the United States and Israel. Intelligence has shown that they have published books on how to build and use weapons of mass destruction. Hezbollah has gained access points along the United States, including the Mexican border to gain entrance into the United States. In a move that we all should support, GOP New York Rep. Pete King has called for Mexican drug cartels to be classified by the Department of Homeland Security as terrorists groups in order to better track their finances and operations. Since these cartels are being trained to build tunnels and shown how to use explosives by the Hezbollah, it only makes sense that these cartels should be labeled as terrorists. It should also be noted that Mexican drug cartel men have been arrested with Farsi tattoos on their shoulders, providing clear indications of how Islamic terrorists are working together with Mexican rebels. However, the most serious threat Hezbollah poses is the merger of operations with the Iranian nuclear program- something which no administration has had the intestinal fortitude to take on. When will we address this situation? Iran's vigorous efforts to become operational have not stopped and are nearing completion. Danger is looming and it is best to take action before it's too late.

Who is Iran?

Voiced through their president and backed by the true leaders of Iran, the Imam's, are determined to reign supreme in the Middle East. Iran has also pledged to wipe the state of Israel off the face of the map. That kind of stance is not good for stability in the Middle East. Add these tidbits to the mix. Iran is a country the size of California, Texas, New York, Michigan and Ohio-combined. Iran's resources include; 75 million people and huge oil reserves. Iran, led by radical Mullahs, has pledged to destroy the United States and Israel, funds and supports Hezbollah in Lebanon, funds Hamas in Palestine and is considered the world's leading sponsor of terrorism. They have been producing ballistic missiles since their war with Iraq in the 1980's and have collected many more missiles since then. These missiles, called Shahab-1, 2 and 3 have range capabilities of 800 miles, enough to reach Israel. Modifications have led to an increase in distance of up to 2000 miles, enough to reach Berlin, Germany. Iran has successfully launched satellites into outer space, providing proof that they have the technology for missal strikes beyond the 2000-mile range and have the power to launch air strikes against the United States. Unfortunately, the Iranian military is capable of striking from launch pads in the ocean, easily reaching the United States. They are buying ballistic and cruise missiles with help from other evil regimes such as North Korea, China and Russia, in order to increase their stockpile of weapons. The processing of uranium will give Iran nuclear capability in next few years and will, no doubt, change foreign policy forever. Allowing a nuclear Iran would be one of the greatest failures in American politics because we are giving into the demands of terrorists. This will create a global danger that will negatively impact not only the United States, but Israel as well. Israel will be at the forefront of this fight and I expect Iran to start a war with Israel as soon as their nuclear arsenal becomes operational. The Bush administration tried threatening Iran and that did nothing. The Obama administration tried sitting down and talking with them -that did nothing. Our only choice is to force their hand. I don't mean starting a war but I do mean a calculated air strike combined with special bunker bombs that would completely destroy their nuclear facilities. It has taken Iran 30 years to come as close as they are in their pursuit of nukes. If the United States were to dismantle Iran's nuclear sites that would buy us at least 15 more years before we would have to deal with this potential catastrophic ordeal again.

There is a race for domination in the Muslim world and Iran intends to win it. Iran's chief rival is Saudi Arabia. Remember this key distinction. Iran is 90% Shiite, the much smaller sect of Islam and Saudi Arabia is 100% Sunni, the dominant sect of Islam. Iran has more people but less oil than Saudi Arabia. Saudi Arabia has a much smaller population; they have more oil and much more support from the rest of the Muslim world. Since 85% of the Muslim world is Sunni, Saudi Arabia has the upper hand. Considering that the two sects absolutely hate each other and will never be in agreement as to which is the true religion of Islam, it can only help the rest of the world. It would be great if they were only concerned with eliminating each other like 2 tigers fighting over a meal. One can only hope…

Enter South America: By using Cuba to further its agenda of world domination that the Soviet Union tried to capture, Venezuela and Iran have fostered a similar relationship in attempting to bring pressure to Israel and America. Venezuela and Cuba continually force the hand of surrounding countries like Brazil, Ecuador, Bolivia and others by using oil as their pressure point. This strain forces those countries to go along with the theocratic dictatorships and ultimately recognize Palestinian as their own independent state. These South American countries are left with the difficult choice of supporting Palestine or losing their energy supply. Iran not only uses South American countries for support of Palestine, but also as a place for positioning purposes. Four and a half billion dollars have been earmarked for operations in Venezuela so that Iran can set up missile bases which have been underway for the past couple years. This is of great concern for the United States because these bases give Iran a strategic retaliatory strike point if they should ever come under attack from the United States or Israel. Iran is gaining a formidable land position and one that America will have to deal with for future operations against them.

It would be one thing if Iran had some sort of hidden agenda but that clearly isn't the case. One does not have to dig too far to unearth quotes from Iran's President: In 2005: "Israel must be wiped off the map." In 2006, "The basic problem in the Islamic world is the existence of the Zionist regime [Israel], and the Islamic world and the region must mobilize to remove this problem." In 2007, "The United States and the Zionist regime of Israel will soon come to the end of their lives." Then in 2009 another quote proving clear indication of their hatred for the United States and Israel: "This regime [Israel] will not last long ... This regime has no future. Its life has come to an end." Iran has said time and time again-Israel does not have the right to exist. They support a Palestinian takeover and routinely chant "death to America." Could the message be any clearer? I think not. It is imperative that Iran does not obtain operational nukes or else the result will be death to hundreds of thousands of innocent men and women. Remember the simple truth for those on the far left who are in denial. If Israel were to lay down their arms and give up their defense, the result would be the death of every single Israeli. However, if the Muslim terrorists groups like Hezbollah, Hamas and their partner Iran were to give up the fight and lay down their rockets, missiles, guns and bombs-the result would be peace. The fact is, Iran continually tells the world that Israel cannot and will not exist.

The call to war is more on the minds of Iran's leaders than anywhere else. The deep-seated belief in the 12th Imam or the Mahdi (a religious prophet to Shia Muslims) is very concerning. However, just because non-Muslims do not think it is true, does not mean they won't try to make it up. The problem is over 90% of Iran is Shiite and over 60% believe in this guy. That comes out to over 45 million people believing in him. Iran's president has already tried to say that 12th imam was here, although he was clearly mistaken. He must be able to take some pretty potent anti-aging pills because he was supposedly born in 868AD. Part of this belief is that this long-lived religious person and Jesus will come back and kill 60-80% of the population or those who have refused to convert to Islam. Why would they ever think Jesus would do that? Jesus saves those who believe in him and his message. What makes things worse is Iran's leaders believe they can hasten the return of this Imam. This includes quickly developing

Iran into a super power to create the right conditions for his coming. See where this is going? Yes, it's going wherever they want it to go, including trying to eliminate anyone who is not Muslim. As the London telegraph reported in 2006, the respected Iranian-born journalist Amir Taheri states that President Ahmadinejad, "Boasts that the [Hidden] Imam gave him the presidency for a single task: provoking a 'clash of civilizations' in which the Muslim world, led by Iran, takes on the infidel's of the West, led by the United States, and defeats it" ("The Frightening Truth of Why Iran Wants a Bomb," *The Telegraph* [London], April 16, 2006). This is why it's so important that Iran never gets a bomb.

Iran supports Hezbollah and Hamas, but they also have close ties to the Palestinian Islamic Jihad in Syria, the Mahdi Army in Iraq, the Al-Aqsa Martyrs Brigades and the Popular Front for the Liberation of Palestine in Gaza and West Bank. Even Iran's own Revolutionary Guard is classified as a terror group by many western governments. It is clear they need to be stopped. We just need the political and social will to stand up and stop the bully from getting what he wants. These are radicals who will say and do whatever it takes for world and religious domination. Common sense based Americans realize no other western nations have the backbone to stand up to these terrorists and that it is up to the United States to take them down. Republicans grasp the enormity of our situation and somehow liberals do not. So far liberals have only shown pacification. Yet, any reasonable person would admit that it is evil to do nothing in the face of evil and the leaders of Iran could not be more evil. They need to be dealt with and it needs to happen now. Maybe other nations will stand up when it affects them more negatively down the road, but by that time it will be too late. The time is now for Israel and the United States to prevent a nuclear Iran. I know we can do it- it is our only choice.

Saudi Arabia

Problem number two is Saudi Arabia. The Saudis are not our friend and never have been. We need them for oil and we want them to fight against

Iran. We sell them arms in exchange for the agreement of oil to be traded in dollars worldwide. This is a very dangerous business relationship we have gotten ourselves into. They are home to the most extreme form of Islam (along side Afghanistan when under the control of the Taliban) in the world known as Wahhabi. Saudi Arabia has the strongest voice (in the Sunni side of Islam) throughout the world because of their vast oil reserves and the fact that the two most important cities in Islam (Mecca and Medina) lie in the sands of Arabia. Our dangerous relationship with Saudi Arabia has allowed them to undermine us through their relentless construction of Wahhabi mosques throughout America, built with oil money and pathetic appeasement by our government. This has allowed the Saudis to slowly but surely infuse their extreme form of Islam into our society. This severe form of Islam has and continues to preach hateful, anti-American messages in 85% of their Mosques. When you have a congregation that gets riled up and worked into frenzy every Friday, sooner or later a radical message gets through. These radical messages inevitably lead some men and women down the wrong path of suicide bombings causing the deaths of innocent men, women and children. Saudi Arabia is using our lukewarm relationship with them to their advantage through the protection of religious freedom we readily grant here in the United States. We need to remember who Saudi Arabia really is and stop pretending that our relationship is cordial.

As previously mentioned, Saudi Arabia promotes the most sever form of Islam anywhere in the world. Sharia Law is the absolute law of the land and it's downright scary. Their form of government is so twisted that it comes right out of the frightening novel, "1984", with spies lurking everywhere making sure their people are kept in line like cattle. Every citizen is forbidden from making any negative statements or judgments against the Saudi government. Writers are put in jail and the heads of government constantly monitor their people. Their censoring ministries are named Supreme Information Council, Press Information Council, Ministry of Information, which are enough to put chills down your spine.

Contradictions are glaringly obvious in the House of Saud. They lavishly enjoy the riches of life more than any other human beings on

Earth. They spend billions on cars, vacations, houses, women, booze – you name it. All this while their own oppressed people are not allowed to enjoy ever the most basic forms of enjoyment. There is zero religious freedom and anyone who leaves Islam, leaves this Earth through murder or kidnapping – never to be seen again. Women are treated worse than slaves. If women are raped they are simply murdered for "allowing" themselves to be dishonored. They must be covered from head to toe at all times outside the home and must never be in public with a man unless they are married. Women have absolutely no life, other than making sure the male is satisfied at home with meals and sex. There is only one way to get ahead in life in Saudi Arabia and that way is through connections -whether that takes place in the form of bloodlines or bribes you must have connections.

The kings have built and continue to finance over 30,000 mosques in Saudi Arabia, which is both impressive and extreme at the same time. For a country that has only 27,136,977 people that's a lot of mosques: About 900 people for every 1 mosque. Then again the Saudi Kings were never that good at managing their money. In fact they have managed to ruin their country faster than most dictatorships throughout history. They are hundreds of billions in debt, a growing population with 30% or more uneducated, 30% barely educated and a lack of available funds to pay for even the basic needs of their citizens. In general the citizens of Saudi Arabia have no freedom, no choices, no job opportunities, no real skills and no true education. Combine all those problems with the fact that they live in an absolute desert with their aquifers drying up…it is like quicksand over there.

Al –Queda, and its leader

A Sunni global terrorists group aimed at destroying the west and Israel in the name of restoring the caliphate. They have been around since 1998 and have been responsible for the death of tens of thousands worldwide including the 1998 US embassy bombings in Tanzania and Kenya, the US embassy bombings in Saudi Arabia, and the horrific terrorist attacks of 9/11.

Al-Queda's origins can be found in the Mujahideen who fought against the Soviet invasion with not only "freedom fighters" from Afghanistan but also with fellow Muslims from around the world who came to the aid of their "brethren" in need. Bin Laden was one of the main financiers who recruited fighters from mosques around the world by inspiring and convincing them that they must deter and remove the Soviets from their land.

Originally, Bin Laden used Saudi Arabia as his main station to set up Al-Queda (the base) and formed the foundation for what is now a world wide terrorist network. After starting in Saudi Arabia, Bin Laden was kicked out of the country for disagreements with the Kings. He then turned to Khartoum, Sudan and made this his real base for Al-Queda. In 1996, his declaration of war against the United States began. He soon realized he needed help and brought other groups in to fortify his plan. He sought out the "International Islamic Front for Jihad Against the Jews and Crusaders" Harakat ul-Ansar, other Egyptian terror groups and many others who were more than willing to help. The group ultimately settled upon Afghanistan as their base after Saudi Arabia pressured Sudan to remove Bin Laden and his fighters. One of his major developments in strengthening the movement was the addition of Egyptian surgeon, Al-Zawahiri. He came from the upper class society of Egypt and was involved with terror since the 1970s. He formed a somewhat uncomfortable relationship with Bin Laden and eventually relocated to Afghanistan to be his top advisor, personal physician, major recruiter and number two in command.

Today Al-Queda's network reaches out like the tentacles of an octopus extending their reach into every corner of the globe including the United States, where, they unfortunately have a real presence. For the most part they work independently but their goal is one in the same. Their aim is to destroy the west and Israel, remove any Christian and Jew from their holy land and to strengthen the global influence of Islam around the world. Any Muslim who is not in agreement with this doctrine is considered an apostate or a person who has turned against Islam. In 1998, Bid Laden's fatwa or call to religious duty was a call to wage a holy war against all Christians and Jews. Their movement in Afghanistan really began to take hold.

How the Taliban came into power

Things started to take a major turn for the worse when the Soviet invasion began. In the 1980's the Mujahideen, who had beaten back the Soviet Union, turned on one another for control. The Taliban leaders, originally from Afghanistan, were educated in Pakistan after fighting against the Soviet Union. They received guidance in Pakistani Madrasses and then returned to Afghanistan looking to establish control through Sharia Law imposed on the people. The purpose was to become the dominant power in Afghanistan, and by this point the country was essentially up for grabs. By 1992, Afghanistan was in complete chaos as competing warlords fought for power. The people of Afghanistan suffered greatly under this chaos, as each warlord had a fief and every fief had a checkpoint. Nothing was off grounds at the checkpoints; women were raped, money was stolen along with beatings and murder. What became a huge problem turned into a disaster as Kabul (the capital) morphed into 42 separate militia checkpoints. The people of Afghanistan were left with no electricity, no visitors, horrific checkpoints, and more war. It is hard to imagine any sort of life with bullets whizzing by and warlords dictating your every move. It became a form of prison, as no one was comfortable leaving his or her home. In an ironic twist of fate, the Taliban seized control over the country that had become like the Wild West. The Taliban became the dominant force and restored order to the chaotic battlegrounds among competing warlords.

Enter the Taliban

After years of warlord street fighting, the Taliban crashed the party. The term Taliban means student and they became a terror group bent on "teaching" their strict and extreme version of Islam on the people of Afghanistan. They emerged on the scene around 1994 while starting off as a group protecting convoys for trade routes. The Taliban were able to keep a stable source of income by smuggling electronics and selling their large quantities of opium. As the Taliban grew in strength, the Afghan people supported them at first because they instituted order to an otherwise lawless place. However, life quickly became much worse as the Taliban sought to inflict their extreme ways of Islamic law. Before long, even the activity of flying a kite was banned! Music was outlawed along with drinking; televisions and colors of any kind were removed and banned. Women had a rough life before the Taliban but now things were really bad. They had to abide by the Sharia law of keeping completely covered. They were not allowed near schools and were murdered for being in public with a male. The Taliban's obsession with enforcing the strictest form of Islam brought the people of Afghanistan back to the 7th century. Even nail polish was forbidden, as a woman could expect to have her finger chopped off for wearing something that would "disgrace her honor."

Modern day Jihad comes from

According to Pulitzer Price winner author, Lawrence Wright, modern day Islamic terrorism stems from a man called Sayyid Qtub. This man was responsible for igniting the agenda of radicalization. Qtub provided the ideological manual "that would echo in the ears of generations of young Muslims who were looking for a role to play in history." The radicalization of Qtub emerges from his visits to the United States, while earning degrees and traveling throughout our country. During his time spent in America he became more and more bothered by the free flinging Americans who were energized by work and play. One could easily see through his writings what a jaded view he had of America and women in general. His Islamic views butted heads with our Christian way of life (since 75% of Americans define themselves as Christians). Wright found some insightful themes in Qtub's writings that helped form the Islamic jihadists that we see today. They include: viewing America as a godless nation, the use of torture and terrorism to steer the masses in the direction of Sharia Law and the obsessive call to purify Islam. The founders of modern jihad have now returned to torture, a form of humiliation, along with deliberate mass murder to carry out their missions. Ayman Al – Zawahiri,founder of the Egyptian terror organization Al-Jihad, was a reader and follower of Qtub. Inspired by Qtub's writings he later became the intellectual driving force behind Al Queda's never-ending quest of returning the country of Egypt to "true Islam." While Qtub's writings got the momentum going, Al-Zawahiri took the ball and ran with it. Al-Zawahiri forged the relationship with Bin Laden because Bin Laden had the money to execute their shared goal of forcing the return of "true Islam" and the retaking of what they see as their "holy lands."

In summary, these insights have left us with three main modern day principles from terrorist: torture as a means of controlling people, returning Islam to its "pure form" and the reclaiming of land that they view as Muslim holy lands. Keeping them at bay won't come easy, but as our great leader, Reagan once said, "Its peace through strength" that will carry the day. In this case it will have to carry the next century or two.

Why do they hate us?

According to the *Politically Incorrect Guide to Islam*, it says in the Koran that all non-believers shall be killed or converted. Fortunately, most Muslims do not really believe this. However, there is no denying what a strong statement that is. Opponents of these strong quotes argue, "Well the bible has some pretty harsh language that can't be justified." That is not a valid point because you don't see Catholics or Christians blowing people up in the name of religion today. This is the Holy War from long ago and radicals hate us because we are infidels. The disheartening part of Islam is that is never forgets and it has plenty of time. This really is the Crusades continuing although no one wants to call it that. We have been at war for thousands of years and the battle rages on.

Radicals hate us because we are not Muslim. What else? Any land that has ever been occupied by Muslims is considered Muslim land from their perspective. What an imperialistic stance! Remember, American haters believe we have been the great oppressor of the world, except it isn't true.

We are the only country in the history of the world that occupies a nation, rebuilds that nation, eliminates totalitarian regimes and then leaves the country. Remember we leave! Every other empire in history invaded foreign land and ruthlessly took it over. The Ottoman Empire reigned from Madrid to the Khyber Pass, dominating a huge chunk of the map for 500 plus years. Why do you think mosques look the way they do? When they captured Holy Christian cities they just added minarets to the top. For instance, Hagia Sophia, the largest Church in Christianity (at that time) was changed from a church to a mosque sometime after 1453 when the Turks captured Constantinople. When Muslim imperialists invaded, killed and conquered the city, they made Hagia Sophia the biggest mosque in the world. I find it very funny how liberal leaders in today's age are so quick to point out America's flaws but seem to ignore oppression and terror committed by radical Islam. So many things you find out in life seem to be the opposite.

The Koran teaches that some day, (the day Allah wants, supposedly) Muslims will be in charge of the whole world. If that is your mentality then, "Houston we've got a problem." The majority of the 311 million Americans do not want to become Muslims, nor do we want to die. Those are our choices when Muslims take over your land. If radicals believe taking over the world is their destiny we are going to have this problem for the foreseeable future. In other words, if you are not one of us, you are against us. For instance, on Seinfeld Show when the Van Buren gang confronted Kramer, he got lucky and flashed the correct gang sign because he was holding the salt and peppershaker with eight digits, as Van Buren was the 8th President. Kramer lucked out on that one. I don't want to be like George Castanza though. He was not so lucky because he wasn't "one of them." Neither are Christians or Jews. If we are not "with them" then we are against them, right? There are a number of teachings that Americans, in particular Christians and Jews, should be very concerned with.

Yes it seems that 90% of Muslims are good and want peace, but all it takes is one. When a religion has over 1 billion believers with 5-10% being horrible, totalitarian, terrorists, then the odds are not good for the rest of the world. 10% of 1 billion is 100 million. That's 1/3 the population of the United States. All it takes is for one of the 100 million to get away with some horrendous act and there would be death, destruction and chaos. Just like 9/11. Let's suppose we are off by 50 million. Meaning all the studies that have been conducted are off by a lot. We still have 50 million terrorists trying to kill, hurt, manipulate and overrun this country. That is a large amount of bad guys.

The Koran's call to War

The Koran has hundreds of verses that call for the believers to wage jihad against those who do not believe. The war is to be against those who reject Islam and those who do not practice the Islam to its fullest. Jihad is the highest duty of a Muslim and the Koran says that paradise is guaranteed to those who "slay and are slain." What about those who say Islam is a religion of peace? They are simply not being truthful with themselves or the public. The Koran indicates that the holy war against non-believers will continue until the world is Islam or the "religion for Allah" is under the hegemony of Islamic Law. Therefore, radical Muslims want the whole world to be under Islamic law. What's more, they make the glaring contradiction that Islam would spread peacefully as long as everyone goes along with the plan and converts to Islam. Well that's bastardizing the word peace. You don't force 6 billion other people on earth (1 billion are Muslim) to become Muslims just because you think they have to convert or else they will go to hell or be killed. That is totalitarian. Since we will not be forced into their religion- the war continues. Radical Muslims use the Koran to justify war against others. Quoting the Koran: "o ye who believe! Take not the Jews and the Christians for your friends and protectors: they are but friends and protectors to each other. And he amongst you that turns to them (for friendship) is of them". Verse 9:5- "slay the idolaters wherever ye find them."

As previously mentioned, the three biggest concerns of Jihad are returning Islam to its pure form, control of religion (and therefore the people) and control of land. Islamic teachings specifically say, any land occupied ever, at any point in history, belongs to Muslims. They believe the land is permanent Muslim land and it's a reflection of their belief in which Allah intends for them to take over these lands. Since, in their eyes, Islam is the perfect social, economic and political vehicle then territories they've conquered happened because Allah wanted it that way. This is an enormous problem we face because it is very hard to argue against the 5-10% of radical Muslims who believe that Muslims shall conquer the world because Allah intends it to be that way. Try telling radicals that Israel belongs to the Jews. The Jews have had a presence in the land of Israel dating back to 13BC, but they don't want to hear about it. Radicals only want to hear what they choose to hear, the teachings in the Koran. Allah wants them to conquer and take over every piece of land. Such is a religion of war, not peace. Those who adhere to the radical version of Islam state that the Koran offers non-Muslims only 3 choices: conversion, subjugation or death. That message dates all the way back to 610AD, yet it remains the same today in 2012. When Muslims are asked, what is the "best deed" one could do besides the act of becoming a Muslim, the Koran says to participate in Jihad (holy fighting) in Allah's cause. Of course these men were and are still offered the best of both worlds. If you fight and are victorious then you receive food, women, fame and riches. If fighters are killed in "holy fighting" they are promised the same earthly treasures in paradise. It's a win- win for them.

What does this all mean?

Jihad terror groups have declared their intention to unify Islamic nations of the world under a single ruler: the caliph. Historically the caliph was the successor of the Prophet as the spiritual and political leader of the Muslims or at least the Sunnis. The caliphate was abolished in 1924 and many contemporary jihadists date the woes of the Islamic world form this date. Jihadists want to restore the caliphate, unite the Islamic world and reinstitute Islamic Law (the Sharia) throughout the world. Although only Saudi Arabia, Iran, and Afghanistan are under Sharia law, modern day Islamic warriors are using jihad to enforce Sharia onto non-Muslim countries though oppression of its citizens. Their societies are backyard and continue to yield nothing in terms of freedom or hope for its citizens.

What about the moderate Muslims who want to live in peace? As I've mentioned earlier only 5-10% of all Muslims remain violent jihad, war -crazy terrorists (although that is still a huge number of people). Yet, making war against non-believers is still the main theme of Islam. The idea of the entire world being peaceful when the whole world is Islamic, is not an option. Even though the Koran instructs believers to take up arms against non-believers there remains millions of moderate Muslims for a couple reasons. For one, there are millions of beautiful, peaceful Muslims who want the same thing as the west- peace. Another reason is that the Koran is written in the classic difficult form of Arabic. Millions know verses and can recite them on command but have no idea of their meaning. We must be mindful that the dangerous, "pure" form of Islam is what the extremists want (most notable, Saudi Arabia and Iran) and we can't let them inform all the other Muslims of the call to war against non-believers. The other reason is that some Muslims refuse to get caught up in the jihadist teachings of the Koran.

The Crusades continued through population shift and oil

There are many accomplishments that we owe to the Muslim world that we might not remember as being so. For example, according to Naill Ferguson in his book, *Civilization*, the first hospital is thought to have come from Damascus, with the help of Al-Waleed bin Abdel Malek in 707AD. The first form of higher education is thought to have originated in Fez around 859, the University of Al- Karaouine. Built from the foundations of Greek and Indians, Muslims established al-jabr, or algebra. We can also thank a Muslim doctor as the first experimental scientist who wrote seven volumes on the book of optics. There are many accomplishments and positive additions that Muslims have given the world from medicine to philosophy to mathematics. As English philosopher Roger Bacon wrote, "Philosophy was drawn from the Muslims." Skipping ahead many hundreds of years later to the fall of the Ottoman Empire, the aftermath of this dominant realm gave way to years of nothingness. The Middle East was dormant, unproductive and stale in terms of global importance. Then the discovery of fossil fuels changed everything. Suddenly a region (and its religion) was forced back into the 20th century by the discovery of fossilized plants. Bacterial decomposition of plants and animals removed most of the oxygen, nitrogen, phosphorus and sulfur from matter, left a sludge made up mainly carbon and hydrogen. Over time, the remains were covered by layers of sand and silt reaching down 10,000 feet while pressure and heat changed the remaining compounds into the hydrocarbons and eventually turning into what we know and use as crude oil, the world's most precious commodity. Because of the decomposed remains of plants and animals the Middle East suddenly had value.

So why does the Arab world, which is in such chaos right now, have a fighting chance against the most powerful army in the world? All one needs to do is look to the west. Here we find one major development: *A population expansion v. a population implosion.* The Arab world is producing far more children than the western world. Also, of great importance is the average age of these children. It is a staggering number but frightening at the same time. What we see is this: Between 1970 and 2000 the developed world's population decreased from roughly 30% to just over 20%, while the Muslim world went from 15% to 20%. That is an incredible shift in only 30 years. As Mark Steyn, author of *America Alone* so rightly put it: "September 11th was not the day that everything changed, but the day that revealed how much had already changed." The implications of this dramatic shift are revealed when one remembers what the ultimate goal for radical Islam is all about: convert infidels, kills those that do not convert and take over the entire world because that is what Allah has intended.

Muslims are in mass exodus to Europe and Canada and they are taking over at an alarming rate. As Steyn points out in his book, *America Alone*, in 2007 there were 53.7 million Muslims in Europe and that's excluding Turkey. Muslims have a huge advantage in population growth. The most popular boys name in Belgium is now, Mohammed. Yet, Muslims are not just outnumbering their counter parts, they have a surging youth population and this points to a Muslim dominated Europe in the coming decades. For instance, in Belgium, 17% of the population is under the age of 18, which will only cause the imbalance to swing more in favor of Muslims. By the year 2050, one in every five Europeans will be Muslim. What has happened to Europe's population? It is pretty straightforward when you stop to consider that Europeans nations simply are not having children. They are too busy enjoying life or marching in protest while screaming unreasonable demands for their pensions in which their governments have absolutely no money to pay for. Another feeble project liberals are heavily invested in is, "saving the planet" from too many people chasing too few resources. Environmentalists have convinced Europeans that the "responsible act" is to have fewer children in order to save mother earth -yeah that's worked out well. Europe will be gone while the Muslims reap the reward of reproducing and enjoying all those fancy buildings and beautiful art. Europeans are getting older and fewer while the Muslim population is expanding and at the same time getting younger. We must remember this point: the youth are the decisive edge and the more you have of them the better off you will be in the coming years. For instance, Spain, Germany and Britain all have a population with less than 20% of its youth under the age of 15. Compare that to Saudi Arabia (dangerous) at 39%, Pakistan (dangerous) at 40% and Yemen (dangerous) at 47%. As previously mentioned, Europeans are not having children for multiple reasons. Too busy, too caught up in pensions, vacation time…but the other major factor of "saving the planet" has really put Europe in a jam. The environmentalists have convinced Europeans that it is responsible is to have fewer children or else some day this planet will be uninhabitable. Paul Erhlic didn't help with his doomsday predictions of the population boom theory that put a scare into every left-winger in the west. His theory along with the tree hugging, dirt eating left, has been that we can no longer sustain this level of human reproduction. These are the same people that told us the earth was going to freeze and that the ice age was upon us only to reverse that theory and tell us, "oh did I say freezing, no I meant melting." These population control freaks told everyone that we are bad, abusive, anti-earthers who are destroying the planet, so stop having sex! Wrong again, its not population that is hurting us but a lack of people. The world will hit a plateau in the year 2050 and then its downhill across the globe. Their basic message was –humans harm the earth and there won't be enough food for everyone. Yet, we quickly found ways to make food more plentiful and it wasn't even that hard. They also told us that oil is drying up and after the year 2000 we are pretty much done. Wrong again! We have so much oil we don't even know what to do with all of it. Whether or not people still believe this liberal lie, it does not detract from the facts we are facing today. Populations are down most everywhere except the Muslim world and some African nations, with no signs of this changing anytime soon. 2.1 is the number to maintain a stable population and American is barely clinging to this mark. Other countries such as Spain (1.1), Ireland (1.9), Canada (1.48), Australia (1.7), Italy (1.2), Germany and Austria (1.3) are failing to even come close. According the Mark Steyn, "Spain's population is being divided in 2 every generation!" This not only means Spaniards are becoming extinct but also they have half as many children as their parents. That's shocking. Right now there are 17 European nations that find their populations halving every 35 years. In all likelihood the population decrease will come quicker because after all, who wants to stick around while waiting on the elderly and paying for their retirement as well. Liberals in America and Europe have taken the bait for environmental extremism hook- line- and-sinker. Conservative folks are procreating at a rate of 12% higher than those on the left. One reason is that we don't believe in the global warming nonsense and another is that conservatives love having children more than liberals. It's worth noting the influx of Latin America has helped put us at the 2.1 per woman mark. If we were to look at only white women's reproduction, the United States falls to 1.85.

There is a lack of purpose, combined with a lack of religious vigor that is especially apparent in Europe. Unfortunately, radical Muslims are preying on these sad impressionable young Europeans. In 2007 young men from Germany, named Fritz and Daniel were arrested just in the nick of time before completing their attack which would have killed as many people as the Madrid and London bombings combined. They had converted to Islam while attending an Islamic center, which was run by a jihadist imam. Remember if you're not with them you're against them.

If Islam were truly a religion of peace, then one might say it's only a shame that Europe's culture was lost to outsiders. However, the loss of Europe's culture won't be the only problem. Europeans will be completely dominated or removed from their land. The burden then falls on America to once again save Europe before it's too late. The problem of population implosion does not just apply to Western Europe. According to Steyn, "Russia is now known as the sick man of Europe." Their population is dwindling faster than you can down a shot of Vodka. They are riddled with AIDS, tuberculosis and 70% abortion rate. Russia has gone from a population 148 million in 1992, to a shocking 130 million by 2015. Their fertility rate is 1.2 children per woman with no signs of stopping. Since you can only expect to live 58.9 years in Russia the rate at which a population dissolves speeds up. Why is this important? Russia is the world's biggest country with an abundance of natural resources. They have too few people with too many resources. Someone is bound to taken advantage of this imbalance and there are a few suspects who are already have their eyes on the prize. China for one has the largest population in the world (1.5 billion) but not enough natural resources. Since eastern Russia is fertile ground with only 10% of their population living in this region -it's ripe for the picking. When you consider the only population sector of Russia that is growing is…you guessed it, Islamic, then only 1 or 2 scenarios are likely. Either China will make a push for that territory or Islamic forces will move in. Also of great concern is the world's largest supply of nuclear arsenal, which will again be up for grabs. So, yes population demographics are vital because you want to continually supply you country with able-bodied young men and women. Europe has obviously forgotten this and the Muslim countries have not. The global race for land and religious domination are becoming extremely dangerous.

Liberal appeasement - Are we fighting more than terrorists?

Slowly but surely we have tried not to think about the terrorist attacks of the past or ones that could occur in the future. We put it to the back of our minds to avoid thinking it could happen again. This is what Obama, his administration and his teams of liberal lawyers are taking advantage of – America's appeasement. While conservatives worry about protecting this great nation, liberals are busy making America defenseless against radical terrorism. One would think there wouldn't be any arguments over the housing of enemy combatants on a tiny island not far from the United States, right? However, the highly dangerous and destructive democrats have campaigned and tried to end the practices that have undermined the security and well being of the United States. Liberals are appeasing radicals because they don't believe we are in a true fight. Obama's termination of enhanced interrogation is a deeply troubling policy. I pray America does not pay the ultimate price of Obama's and his administration's nearsighted destructive decision-making. The liberal policy of sending in teams of liberal lawyers concerned with "justice" for terrorists, pro bono is what America is up against. These liberal lawyers come in with their fancy suits and enormous egos telling the terrorists just what to say to get them back on the battlefield. We have released and fought against over 400 captured terrorists as of 2009! That is downright destructive. These are military combatants. Terrorists should not be offered normal rights of an American citizen let alone have the help of accomplished lawyers working and being paid with our tax dollars in order to release them! Every time these liberal lawyers perform their pro bono work, they endanger the lives of our men and women on the battlefield. They are working against our soldiers. If you remember nothing else from this book remember this: Because of President Bush's implementation of detainees at Guantanamo Bay and his intestinal fortitude to use enhanced interrogation techniques and we have obtained extremely important, sensitive and truthful information from captured enemy combatants. These tactics have undoubtedly saved your life and the lives of your family and friends. Also, just as important to remember: Democrats and Obama have removed the necessary tactics of interrogating terrorists making life much more dangerous for every American. Waterboarding is an effective and safe technique that provides us with highly sensitive information. The terrorists have said so themselves. Unless they go through uncomfortable procedures they will not give up information. Terrorists have said, without any reservation, that their holy book says it's ok to reveal information only after enduring feats that test their mind and body. If we go into their jail cell and say "hey guys, we'd really like some info, how about it," we will never obtain any information. Terrorists need to be tested. They have said so themselves. Also, if waterboarding were so terrible than investigative journalists would not have volunteered to try it out as they have over the years. Torture is not something you just try out. For instance, no one says, "yes rip off my finger nails I want to see if it really hurts." Waterboarding is about making you very uncomfortable. It is 100% necessary and it saves lives by obtaining reliable intelligence. Liberal appeasement of sending in lawyers to get terrorists out of jail along with the stopping of enhanced interrogation techniques by liberals and Obama, could go down in history has the most anti-American, dangerous, bizarre policies every instituted. Obama and his cronies have taken our sword and shield away, handcuffed our soldiers' wrists together and said go fight the enemy. If you are to somehow subdue him don't get any information from him, because we will find a way to prosecute you back "home."

Below are ten important points to remember according to highly acclaimed author, Marc A. Thiessen of *Courting Disaster*. His groundbreaking research presents remarkable insight to the success that Republicans have had at defending this great nation and the colossal failure with which Democrats are setting the United States up for with their liberal appeasement of terrorists.

1. Terrorists don't fall under Geneva Convention, they are enemy combatants, and they don't get the treatment that Geneva Convention offers. Terrorists have no rights under Geneva because they wear ordinary clothes, hide among civilians and endanger the innocent. Giving them rights undermines the very purpose of the Geneva Conventions. Additionally, Common Article 3 was really put in place to protect innocent civilians so that violations of law during times of war could be stopped or prevented.

2. It has been shown that enhanced interrogation techniques have saved American lives. Detainees have knowledge of future attacks, many of which target innocent civilians. The information we extrapolate provides safety to civilians against future terror strikes. The enhanced interrogation techniques used on KSM (Kalid Sheik Mohammed) stopped the "Bojinka Plot" which would have murdered over 4,000 innocent civilians in 7 different planes. This and many more plots have been prevented because of interrogation of terrorists. Of the 80,000 terrorists captured fewer than 800 were moved to Guantanamo Bay for detention and interrogation. An even smaller number were taken into CIA custody, about 100 in all.

3. Waterboarding has been used on over 26, 829 men in our military. If water boarding were torture we never would have used it to train our own military. The definition of torture is having something done to you that you do not want to happen. If waterboarding is so bad then why do journalist and television reporters go and "try it out" to see what its like. Waterboarding is nothing. Having your fingernails ripped out and have boiling water poured over your entire body- now that is torture.

4. We've only used enhanced interrogation techniques on 29 detainees. There was also strict oversight. Every technique had to be approved in advance by headquarters and any deviation would mean removal of the interrogator. Admiral McConnell said he admires President Bush for having the courage to authorize enhanced interrogations following the 9/11 attacks. He made a heroic decision. It saved lives and probably prevented another attack.

5. Guess who has done away with the enhanced interrogations that have protected American lives everyday: The Obama administration.

6. Interrogating terrorists at Guantanamo Bay is wonderful because it has stopped future attacks. Guess how many have been waterboarded at Gitmo, ZERO!

7. Guess what the far left liberal lawyers who now work in the Obama administration do? They work for free trying to release hardcore

crazy radicals. These liberal lawyers also pass notes for detainees to others enemies on the battlefield, endangering the lives our troops.

8. Obama decided to release the Justice Department memo showing all the terrorists how to defeat our very weak definition of enhanced interrogation- incredibly dangerous. Why would he do this? In my opinion, that is a treasonous act coming from the President of the United States of America. Now terrorists know their options and can just wait us out. They have already translated the new rules into Arabic and are telling each other how to defeat us and what to expect when caught. All they really have to do is ask for a liberal lawyer. These are the most ridiculous acts of appeasement I've ever seen. I never thought after 9/11, that leaders of America would go out of their way to help terrorists defeat America.

9. Obama, his admin and liberal lawyers have debased the morale of our intelligence community. Liberals have handcuffed our military and made their job harder while at the same time increased the likelihood of terrorists returning to the battlefield.

10. Obama says that enhanced interrogation at Guantanamo Bay actually serves as a recruiting tool for our enemies. This fact is completely false and here is why: There weren't any prisoners from the war against Afghanistan or Iraq that were being held at Guantanamo Bay before 9/11. Nor was there any CIA interrogation program when the terrorists tried to bring down the World Trade Center in 1993, or when they blew up our embassies in Kenya and Tanzania, or when they attacked the USS Cole, or when they attacked us on 9/11. Obama and liberals always make excuses for terrorists, but evil always finds ways to justify their cause. Those evil bastards can site many reasons for jihad, but none of their reasons ever match what our far left president and his team of czars ever say. Remember, successful terrorist attacks are what get new terrorists to join, not Guantanamo Bay and CIA interrogations.

It's hard enough fighting one or two terrorist groups. Yet, we have much more than one or two groups to overcome. We have to fight against al-Queda, Hezbollah, Hamas, the Taliban, Pakistan (secretly fighting us) and Iran. We must also watch out for Russia, who continually supplies terrorists groups with weapons and bombs along with Saudi Arabia who finances terrorist plots around the world, North Korea (nuclear arsenal), China's military force being the largest in the world as well as Venezuela and Syria. That's around 12 very dangerous problems out there in the world and the United States is the only one capable of dealing with all of them. We definitely have a lot of work left to accomplish.

What we can do to stop Islamic Terrorism
We can help ourselves by…stop appeasing terrorists!

We have survived the attacks of radical Islam so far because of the strategies implemented by George W. Bush. Thank you so much President Bush! His brilliant application of attacking the enemy has indeed helped keep us safe. By taking the fight to the enemy we put the pressure on them. Additionally, our troops have continued to keep us safe by engaging the enemy abroad instead of waiting for attacks at home. We have made it harder for terrorists to communicate, raise money, train soldiers and move from country to country. We have put pressure on the terrorists by implementing the likes of Guantanamo Bay, military commissions, indefinite detention, the Patriot Act and enhanced interrogation techniques. These have allowed us to gather critical, truthful, life saving intelligence that has protected America.

Let us remember that the fight against radical Muslims is just beginning. They do not look at this fight as a 5 or 10 or even 15-year war. This is a century-long war, maybe more. This could go on for hundreds of years. This is a war of ideology, in which radicals believe with every fiber of their being, that Islam is the religion that is supposed to dominate the world. To them, it is God's ultimate mission and it is their job to carry out that mission. The sooner we acknowledge this the better off we will be. Radical Muslims are perfectly content to sit back and take slow bites at our society in many different forms. Sure, they want to attack us with weapons, that's a given. But they are equally satisfied to allow the threat of an attack to constantly remain on our radar. Another goal of terrorism is to let us fight amongst ourselves. We have become so obsessed with making sure we show enormous political correctness for the enemy. We go out of our way to give them lawyers, who then get them back on the battlefield to fight us again. Liberals have shown other outrageous attempts at appeasement by trying to give captured terrorists the same rights as American citizens. Perhaps the biggest mistake we have made is to let liberals dictate our enhanced interrogation of captured terrorists. Khalid Sheikh Mohammed proved to be the biggest capture in the war on terror. He showed to be the toughest son of bitch amongst them all. However by using waterboarding, sleep deprivation, tough physical moves and other techniques we were able to get **credible, highly important information from him through those techniques.** Terrorists are unlawful combatants against the United States. The only thing so irritating is that these terrorists have it way too good! They gain an average of 22 pounds at Gitmo. These terrorists are routinely given time for soccer and enjoy specially prepared meals in accordance with their diet and Islamic teachings. Oh and they do have an occasional fight…over the lazy boy chairs provided for them. One enemy combatant, who was transferred from Guantanamo Bay to an American jail, quickly asked for a return to Gitmo. Now that is saying something. The fact that America's left is so concerned whether or not we might offend or rough up some terrorists who want to hurt and kill us is beyond reason. Maybe the only solution is let overly concerned liberals share some time with them at Gitmo. We'll see how much concern liberals have for terrorists after that. Terrorists want to kill us and liberals want to protect them. It is the most offensive, backwards, weird, confusing notion I've ever come across.

Dividing America

Any fair-minded person must admit that our problem of unity is mainly due to liberals and their agenda of political correctness and appeasement. Think about it. During the traumatic events of 9/11, we were all joined together by a common enemy bent on destroying America. Nothing has changed in that respect. Radicals still want to destroy us, but now we are fighting amongst ourselves. This division has occurred through a lack of common sense and the anti war agenda of the left. It is safe to say 95% of America was for retaliation of those cowardice attacks. However, because war is a long and difficult struggle, certain groups in America took advantage of this. Of course, no one wants one single person in our military to perish, but in times of war that is an unfortunate truth. When men and women in our military began dying, liberals in America began using their deaths as a political ploy to divide the nation on whether or not we should continue to hunt down radical terrorists that want to destroy America. Then the problem of finding weapons of mass destruction started. It seemed as though liberals in America where hoping for this all along. Because we couldn't find any WMD's in Iraq, liberals went nuts! The fact remains that Iraq was a threat. In all likelihood Russia moved those WMD's and placed stockpiles in Syria and some in Russia. Since the weapons inspectors weren't allowed to look anywhere else and the enemy was given all the time in the world to relocate the weapons, it's no wonder we never found any in Iraq. Despite liberating Iraq, capturing a terrorist dictator that had killed more Muslims than any other person in modern history and used chemical weapons on his own people…somehow this wasn't enough for those on the political left. Then the vitriolic rhetoric of making George Bush into a war criminal began. This was really the breaking point in our unity. I believe when the liberal citizens of America showed their hatred of our President who was doing everything he could to keep us safe (and did) this was what started our division. The anti war left divided America between those who supported going after the enemies who had waged war against America and those who thought we should do nothing, again. The left spewed hatred at George Bush and Dick Cheney making them out to be blood- thirsty war criminals. Those terrible insults and lies lead to a push back against them and the division in America was back. Further escalating the problem was the subject of enhanced interrogation, a topic that was highjacked by the left. They claimed to be morally superior and that anything used to get information from terrorists was deemed unacceptable. We continue to che cause of the very same enemy obsessed with destroying us. We up them by building mosques, removing interrogation techniques, not enforcing stricter immigration policies and making it harder to spy on them. We allow supporters of our enemies to teach anti American and anti Israeli rhetoric in our universities, filling the minds of our youth with toxic garbage. I believe these are the fundamental steps for letting the enemy overtake us. Liberal appeasement has made it easier for terrorists to plan terrorist attacks on America and it has got to stop.

We must call the enemy what it is.

We must find ways to make Islamic radicals lay down there arms. If anyone has any better idea other than taking the fight to them, please let me know. As Khomeini said in 1979, "Muslims must rise up in this struggle." "A struggle between all nonbelievers and Muslims." Or as the now dead Bin Laden said, "This war is fundamentally religious. Under no circumstances should we forget this enmity between us and the infidels. For the enmity is based on creed."

We all must acknowledge that there is a war. The war is about religion, power and the ability to dominate the other side. Radicals believe that Allah has chosen them to rule the world and that Islam is the chosen religion. Acceptance of this fact will help us move forward and come to the realization that indeed our very way of life, our religious and political freedom will be gone if we do not defend ourselves against radical Islam. America's hope in surviving lies not in pacifism, but in our strength to defend this great nation.

Reform of Islam

Firmly planted in the minds of Americans is the idea that we should be above making judgments about other countries and their religions. Even when those countries defile women, rape and kill women for no reason, oppress homosexuals, attack and kill Jews and attack innocent men and women – somehow we are still not supposed to judge? Are you kidding me? Of course we are supposed to judge. It is obvious that radical Islam causes the destruction, death and fear in this world. Not every Muslim is a terrorist, but almost every terrorist is a Muslim. There is just no getting around this fact. What we need from moderate Muslims is the ability to stand up and fight for what is right. With radical Islam there is only oppression, hardship and murder. There is no fun, period. Gone are games to play. Gone are colors in clothes and buildings. Gone is music of any kind. You are not even allowed to fly a kite. Your freedom is stripped away in every sense. According to a 2010 Freedom House survey, of the world's 47 Muslim majority countries, only 2 are free! The only explanation is the political suppression of Islam upon its people. There is no separation of church and state and Sharia law rules the land. Muslims must see the light and be willing to stand up for democracy in the face of ruthless dictatorships. All around the Middle East Christians and Jews are treated like outcasts in these societies. They are not even close to having the same equality that Muslims do. Now look at America. Everyone is free. You are not oppressed living here as a Muslim. You are free! How many of us would pack up and go for a vacation to Iran? Of course no one, because you could be locked up forever for doing nothing! We have no rights there. Islamic countries must step up and allow for equal rights in their countries for non-Muslims.

The rejection of science has put Muslim scientific accomplishments back to the stone ages. Saying everything happened because Allah willed it to be is naïve. In Islam law of physics no longer apply. Shooting an arrow into an apple that was lying upon someone's head didn't happen because of the shooters aim or gravity under Islam. It happened because Allah willed it. Maybe, maybe not. Taking science or physics out of consideration is a simpleton's view of the world. One in which you miss out on the wonders of the planet. The rejection of women's rights in all Arab nations must be reformed for Islam to move forward. Islam has not moved forward for centuries and continues to persecute women, essentially giving them zero rights. Women in America don't walk around in those black -death robes,

Just think about how hot they must be walking around in a desert covered in sheets from head to toe, barley breathing. That alone is oppression.

Oppression is also not being able to hold hands with a man in public if you are not married to him. That is not living a free life. If a woman wants to leave her life of subjugation, she is not allowed to do so. They are hunted down and murdered if they try. Women are basically slaves under Islam and lead a scary, boring, extremely hard life. The double standard for men to behave any way they like while women are stoned to death is not the way society should function. It goes against every fundamental right a human being should have and Islamic nations do not afford those rights, especially to women.

The last main idea that Muslims need to address is the obsession with Israel. How many times can you talk about it? Get over it. Leave Israel alone and move on with you lives. Even if Israel stole that land from the Muslims – which Israel did not- why are so many radicals obsessed with that little piece of land? It is like a child who has a giant cookie and he sees another child with a little tiny cookie. The child cannot get over the fact that someone else has a cookie and never enjoys what he has. As professor Khan of Delaware University has said, "Islam is not about defeating Jews or conquering Jerusalem. It is about mercy, about virtue, about sacrifice and about duty. Above all, it is the pursuit of moral perfection." Reform for Islam can happen. I pray it happens. I pray that we do in fact, have a world of peace. Perhaps one day we will be able to wake up without the threat of radicals plotting to destroy the west. Who wouldn't love to wake up to feelings of safety, happiness and peace? If Islam truly is the religion of peace, please show it. Actions are more powerful than words, so please do something about it. Up till now all we've seen is destruction of this beautiful world. What we all want is peace and it starts with Islam. The pieces are there, your move...

R is for "Reforming" Health Care

Remember the words of Obama when he said this: "No matter how we reform health care, we will keep this promise to the American people." "If you like your doctor, you will be able to keep your doctor, period. If you like your health care plan, you'll be able to keep your health care plan, period. No one will take it away, no matter what."

It turns out this will not be the case heading into 2014. In fact one could say this was his plan all along. If Obama couldn't pass a single payer system with a filibuster majority congress, whom could he ever do it with? Remember, the average cost for an employer to provide health care for one employee is around $8,000 and for a family the cost is nearing $16,000. This is not only a matter of importance for each person's medical care but also a huge financial imposition on small business owners (which is 70% of America) because medical costs continue to rise. The Obama administration has introduced legislation as part of Obamacare that will force companies to offer healthcare or face a fine. Since the fine is much less than what you would pay in current costs, take a wild guess as to what companies plan to do. Yep, they will be dropping your health coverage. And why wouldn't they? In 2014, when companies drop their employees, the employees will be forced to rely on government subsidies. Now guess who gets to pay for that? Yep you got it right again, you the taxpayer. It is basically impossible to say how many companies plan to drop their health insurance, but it's safe to say that many will indeed make the move. This is exactly what Obama intended all along. In a 2008 debate, Obama said, "If I were designing a system from scratch, I would set up a single-payer system." We the American people are ultimately left with the single –payer system after a few years. Why should companies keep their health insurance and pay enormous amounts of money when they can just pass the bill down the line like everyone else?

What will Obamacare do?

Obamacare will increase the cost of medical care- you can bet on that. You can't have the government (which is already at the edge of a financial cliff) add *at least another 1.76 trillion* dollars of debt and not expect increases to the taxpayer. Americans can expect rationing of care (especially for the elderly), dramatic increase in waiting times (what used to take 1 week will now take 3 –6 months) to see the doctor or schedule a procedure. Panels will tell you if or when you qualify for surgery. These panels will be comprised of 12-16 person groups responsible for determining your fate. If you plan on doing anything, you had better start booking your surgery before 2014. What else can we expect? We can expect fewer doctors choosing medicine as their profession as well as cutbacks in the treatment of diseases and a reduction in inventions. The use of older technology will become the norm, which will affect businesses that supply medical technology and inevitably force medical businesses to shut their doors. People will not know when or if treatments will be covered. America's healthcare system is going to be chaotic. All these changes come at a time, when most countries have been rethinking their socialized medicine platform and are trying to merge into the private sector again. The greatest place on Earth to receive medical care will be no more starting in 2014. This is the scariest time in the history of America's health system.

Obamacare winners and losers

Unless Obamacare gets repealed, it is pretty clear that the true winner in all of this is big government. When big government takes over, the handouts begin especially to unions and large corporations. Many unions and large-scale corporations were granted the choice to "opt out" of Obamacare to the tune of 1,472 companies. It is ironic how that happened, since many of those 1,472 companies were campaign donors to Obama. These well-connected companies were happy to support Obamacare in spirit as long as they were able to opt out. Unions received 50% of the waivers and yet comprise of only 12% of the American workforce. It pays to have friends in high places...

Unfortunately we the American people lose. We lose because government has control over our healthcare. We lose because we will experience a decrease in quality of healthcare combined with increase costs in the form of additional taxes. A new 3.8% healthcare tax will apply to home sales over $250,000 and sadly that is just the beginning. We will be forced to pay that extra 3.8% tax on investment income, capital gains, dividends, rent and royalties. Another negative is the 2.5% tax on income for failing to enroll starting in 2016. More shortcomings in Obabamcare apply to itemized medical deductions. Under Obamacare, the percentage at which an individual could claim a deduction rises from 7.5% to 10%; just another way for our behemoth government to stick his unwelcome hand in your wallet. With America's debt increasing at over $41,000 per second, the only solution Democrats come up with... more spending! In 2006 and 2007 we had 4.5% unemployment. By 2011 and 2012, Democrats said the budget deficits would be cut in half. Every percentage increase in Americas Gross Domestic Product above the Congressional Budget Office's baseline is worth 3 trillion dollars in lower deficits over 10 years. Recall Obama's promise to the American people, "We're going to reduce costs to an average of $2,500 per family on premiums." It is wonderful that we inventions like video cameras because when prices sky rocket we can go back and hit the replay button. Eighty-seven percent will see premiums rise by an average of 41% in the individual market. Government cannot just add millions and expect premiums to drop by 1,000s of dollars per family. Government control has and always will be at odds with the free market, because government does not have to answer to anyone.

Democrats have proposed...

Well let us see...Democrats have been hysterically yelling that the Republican plan put forth by Paul Ryan would kick granny out into the streets by eliminating Medicare and by making cuts (although necessary). Democrats are simply wrong again. Obama applied cuts to Medicare in the tune of 500 billion and re-applied this to the Obamacare deficit. You can't make the same cut apply twice! Even though Democrats cut 500 billion from Medicare for their healthcare monstrosity, they say Republicans are kicking granny to the curb. Not the case! Paul Ryan's plan does not change one thing for those people 55 and older. Not one thing. For those 55 and younger you will have a choice. You can pay way more in Medicare in the form of mandatory taxes and altered plans or you can choose the Republican plan concerned with saving America's health care system and eliminating endless, destructive spending.

Democrats and Obama were determined to pass healthcare reform regardless of public support. This new healthcare bill was forced down our throat without any clear picture of how to pay for it, or any type of coverage details. Polls show that, indeed, this is true. At least 63% of Americans are against this socialized medicine plan. Each day numerous special interest groups are lobbying for exemptions to this bill because they do not want inferior health insurance at a higher cost. This big government bill was passed without team Obama fully grasping how it will be funded. Take for instance, the portion of the bill that was supposed to fund long-term care. This is called the CLASS Act or Community Living Assistance Services and Supports Act and it was removed from the bill in the fall of 2011. In a strange twist, 40% of the savings in Obamacare were to come from the CLASS Act, saving trillions, according to the Congressional Budget office. Yet, this same portion of the bill, which was supposed to save up to 40%, was removed because the CLASS Act would have put an even greater financial strain on America's healthcare. Not only did Democrats not care, they tried to jam the long-term care portion of the bill through while knowing full well just how damaging it would be to the American people. Thankfully, Republicans were able to insert a provision making it impossible for that portion of the bill to go forward if it did not provide proof of its financial stability. Spendocrats, I mean Democrats, are willing to pass bills that will cause economic hardship just so that they can show their base that they did it – pandering for votes. This is yet again, another example of the profound arrogant, inept, childish nature that is the Democratic Party.

What's in the bill?

Remember one of the most idiotic quotes in political history by Nancy Pelosi? "We have to pass the bill to find out what's in it." Haha. Really, is that how it works? I don't think so. It is hard enough to get a straight answer out of Washington, let alone relying on bills being passed without knowing what's in them. So what is in this enormous 2,700-page bill? Liberals want you to think Obamacare is looking out for your best interests, but it is obviously not. All the rhetoric and talking points make it seem like this is the greatest thing since sliced bread. Everyone's getting health insurance, even though, technically everyone already has health insurance as no one can be denied care at the hospital. It is unfortunate but the America people have been served some bad tasting medicine in the form of misleading information purposely put forth by liberals and this administration. Starting with the lie that costs will go way down. That truly would be magical, but it's mathematically impossible to produce. Obamacare will cost the American people ***at least*** 1.76 trillion dollars more. Another lie forced upon us was the repetitive statement by the Obama administration that, "you can keep your current insurance no matter what." This is simply not the case at all as government will take away the ability of private companies to compete with the government through subsidies and fines. The decree of big government is here and is ushering in the age of socialized medicine to the detriment of the American people. Not only will panels of government paid workers be deciding when you are eligible for surgery, they may state you are ineligible in the first place. Why are we going the way of Europe's failed experiment of socialized medicine since we've seen that it doesn't work? Competition for new drugs will disappear, as government will be the only game in town, reducing the ability for companies to compete over producing new advances in medicine. While we are at it, good luck in finding more students to pursue a career in medicine since they will be paid less, have less say in patient care and have less access to helpful drugs because of government's monopoly over the industry.

What happens when government tells you what to do? Welcome to the wonderful world of mandates. In 1979 there were only 252 mandates put in place giving an average of 5 per state. In 2009 America had 2,133 mandates or an average of 42 per state. Why should we be expected to purchase the same coverage when the needs of each individual vary wildly from person to person? For instance, it is ridiculous to mandate that a 22 year old just out of college must carry an expensive full coverage health care plan. Most people that age cannot afford $350/month health insurance coverage. Especially since a typical 22-year old male does not need to go to the doctor very often and would really benefit from purchasing a catastrophic policy for only major situations to keep costs down, while still having protection. Obviously a 22-year-old male does not need maternity coverage but he will be forced to buy this coverage under the new healthcare law. Of course Obamacare will forbid (by federal law) citizens to purchase low cost minimum coverage. It must fulfill "minimum coverage standards." By forcing these mandates upon the American people this will drive up the cost of insurance by making insurance companies cover a wide range of treatments and conditions. Considering that these mandates will force premiums up by 10.5% (on average) across the United States it creates an additional $1,300 onto each employer sponsored health plan. Not only that but since Obamacare is getting rid of co- payments on preventative care you can bet that cost will be made up somewhere and that "somewhere" will end up in your premium.

Instead of focusing on real change that actually helps the American people, we are left with increased premiums and crushing health care mandates that will usher in the demise of our healthcare system. In summary you can't make healthcare a "one size fits all commodity." People are different and have different needs that fit their situation. Plus people's lives change so why should we be forced to buy the same insurance policy that someone else may want when it won't benefit your life just because the government mandated it. Once government digs its claws into the fabric of a society it becomes entangled upon the cloth and refuses to let go.

America deserves better. We deserve better than the 21 new taxes that will be implemented by Obamacare, passed by the Supreme Court in late June 2012. Twelve of which will hit people making less than $200,000 a year -something Obama promised would never happen. We will be given one more chance to repeal this disaster if we can elect Mitt Romney for President in November 2012. Hopefully through hard work and legislative reform of Obamacare it can still be stopped before it destroys and ruins healthcare in 2014.

Reduce cost? Improve quality? Provide it for all?

We need real ideas for health care reform. Real solutions for the way we receive health care, the drugs that are available, when you receive care, decisions on eligibility, the length of time it takes to see a doctor, the quality of care that you receive and the total cost. A Rasmussen survey of 1,000 voters in May 2010 showed that 63% want Obamacare repealed and that repeal can happen. The American people need to know what they are up against. Unfortunately this new health care bill is 2,700 pages long but does not address any changes that benefit the American people. Most everyone can agree that America does indeed, need real healthcare reform. However, reform can happen through private sector, not in a big government takeover. There is a reason why diplomats across the globe come to the United States when their health is in peril. We have the best resources, best drugs, best medical equipment and the highest quality doctors who provide the very best care.

Just so no one has amnesia, let us reiterate what Mr. Obama said over and over again during his campaign and then during his push for this legislation. Here are some quotes from Mr. Obama: his plan would "Cut the cost of a typical family's premium by up to $2500 a year." Another one was, "If you like your current health insurance, nothing changes, except your costs will go down." He intends to cover everyone's health insurance while at the same time lowering the cost of insurance for everyone. He thinks he can manipulate prices (sounds like central planning?). He also stated that he would improve our quality of health care. "We must redesign our health system to reduce inefficiency and waste and improve health care quality, which will drive down costs for families and individuals. Sounds like a tall order: reduce cost, improve quality and provide it for all. How does he intend to do such a thing?

For starters, he begins by forcing every American to purchase health insurance. This idea has come under a large amount of scrutiny because it is unconstitutional. Currently we are all waiting for the Supreme Court to rule on whether or not Obama and his czars will be able to change our constitution and force us all to buy socialized healthcare. If you don't purchase this health insurance mandate you will be fined. Like the Gestapo coming to your door to collect their money from you despite not doing anything, so will be the role of the IRS showing up at your doorstep making you pay your fine from the government. Next, Medicaid will take on an extremely big increase that will see an additional 18 million people added to the other 34 million currently in the system of "free" government insurance. Another area of big government manipulation will lead to a reduction of care. You can't add 45 million people (or so) to a system and not ration care. Regulation then kicks in by forcing the hand of insurance companies. The government will tell each insurance company what they can include in their coverage along with how much they can pay out in claims. In essence, free market principles will disappear because big government has kicked them out!

There will be such an increase in bureaucracy of administration, regulation, consultants and so-called experts telling you, the patient, how much care, what drugs you get and how much per claim is paid out, that the idea of having your own insurance goes completely out the window. As early as 2013 (which is right around the corner) an individual with an income over $200,000 a year and families making more than $250,000 will be stuck with Medicare payroll tax increase. Essentially Obama will be handing people hidden taxes through a 3.8% tax on unearned income including capital gains, dividend income rental income and more. Also, you can expect an increase in regulation on using Health Insurance Saving Accounts because of government policies dictating the amount one can use in their Flexible Spending Accounts. All told Obamacare will be handing the American people 21 additional taxes totaling over 500 billion plus in just taxes.

Reducing cost of insurance for every American: How can we do this when we are adding 45 million people to the system? Remember, nothing in life is free and this will still be the case with Obamacare. Drugs, machines and supplies cost money and so do doctors, nurses and staff personnel. If these things cost billions of dollars why would "free" health care be labeled as such? Moving your health care from your current plan to the central planners of the government will guarantee an increase in costs. Rationing of care is 100% certain. Unfortunately for the American people there will be other certainties. There will be drug shortages, massive increases in wait time combined with huge decreases in the quality of care one receives. Canada reported 694,161 people who were on a waiting list for surgeries and other treatments in 2009. As the years go by the waiting time goes up. Waiting time has more than doubled since 1993 and has no sign of letting up. In 2009 the median national wait time for a CT scan was 4.6 weeks. I don't know about you but I've never come close to waiting that long for a scan. After getting into a scary "accident" in 2004 I had a CT scan a few days later. That, my friends, is one of many differences you'll find between healthcare in the United States and socialized medicine throughout the world. Another difference comes at the expense of technology. We will see old technology continue to get older. The Fraser Institute, the European Coordination Committee of the Radiological and Electro medical Industries state that no more than 10% of health technology should be older than 10 years. Pretty much nothing in Canada meets this measure. This is not surprising. The United States has the latest and greatest technology that continues to help detect and prevent disease for our citizens. Additionally, research has shown that doctors want to leave the socialized healthcare in their own countries. Who can blame these doctors for leaving if you are guaranteed to make less? For instance, doctors earn only 42% in Canada, what they could make in the United States. Why would you stay? Maybe you have such pride in your country that you are willing to take that automatic pay decrease and stay home. That's very nice of you. The rest of the doctors in Canada don't see it that way. Canada ranks 26/30 for the number of doctors per 1000 according to the Organization for Economic Cooperation and Development. Before the government took over they were 4th. Another symptom of Obamacare will be a decrease in quality of care. I'm from the Midwest and I take pride in the fact that the Cleveland Clinic is one of the greatest hospitals in the entire world. Since I've had my fair share of injuries, I thought it was worth the long drive to travel over five states in order to see doctors at the Cleveland Clinic, while sharing hospital time with diplomats from other countries who chose our healthcare over their own socialized medicine. The list is long- from so called princes in the Middle East to Prime Ministers in Europe. In 2006, Prime Minister Silvio Berlusconi traveled to an American hospital for heart surgery instead of going with the "free" nationalized health care in Italy.

I think by now we've all heard the horror stories of nationalized health care from Cuba, Canada, England and virtually anyone else out there. Ian Boynton, a former soldier in England, was forced to pull out 13 of his teeth with a pair of pliers after 30 attempts at finding a dentist failed. Or on a national level, according to Britain's National Health Service, they cancelled around 100,000 operations in 2008 and more than 1 million Brits are waiting to be admitted to hospitals. Pay attention to England because we are modeling our socialized medicine in the exact same manner as the Brits.

What about cheaper drugs in socialized medicine countries? Yes it's true you can obtain some drugs for cheaper amounts in other countries. The only reason drugs are cheaper is because their governments impose price controls to accomplish this. Of course who keeps those prices down low - the taxpayer. Drugs are kept low through price controls, which mean supplies are limited. In the case of England, the NHS denies the newest drugs to citizens when they consider them unnecessary. Government intrusion always results in limited access to drugs and the rationing care by eliminating competition. The National Institute of Health and Clinical Effectiveness (NICE) gets to decide which treatments the NHS will cover. For instance, when Americans were greatly relieved to receive the wonder drug Gleevec, England was left out in the cold (or rain). It took *NICE* 2 years to even say they would supply it. By that point, as we all know, 1000's suffered or passed away from leukemia in England. In 2005 the drug, Tarceva, was being used throughout Europe. However, NICE determined that the drug was just too expensive for England, despite study after study showing how this drug greatly prolonged the life of cancer patients.

Cancer is a horrible disease. Take a guess at who leads the world in treating it. You got it, the United States of America. Because Canadians and Europeans are the only ones worth comparing, the Lancet Oncology study in 2008 found that the United States has a better survival rate for 13/16 of the most common cancers five years of diagnosis. Always check the numbers. Many haters of the United States don't want to paint the United States in favorable light. One can see this was the case on the important issue of life expectancy. In 2007 the United States reached a rating of 77.9 according to the Centers for Disease Control and Prevention. This study showed the United States behind 30 other countries. Among some of the countries ahead of the United States were Sweden, France, Hong Kong, Canada, as life expectancy is well beyond 80 years in those countries. Because many love taking shots at the United States, this is just another case of trying to paint the kettle black. Life expectancy takes on so many factors not just health care or infant mortality. It includes homicide rates, accidents, diets and ethnic diversity among many other factors. Unfortunately, the United States has a higher homicide rate and a higher rate of accidents- 5.9% and 14.24 respectively. Not surprisingly, Americans who don't die in homicides or car accidents outlive every other country. The World Health Organization (WHO) defines a live birth as any infant that once removed from its mother, breathes or shows any other evidence of life such as beating of the heart, pulsation of the umbilical cord or definite movement of voluntary muscles. Yet, the United States counts all births regardless of births weight or prematurity. Sadly in Switzerland, an infant must be at least 30 centimeters long at birth to be counted as living. That's pretty pathetic. In France if your baby is less than 26 weeks it's registered as dead. Therefore, fewer babies are "counted" as alive, so fewer babies are "counted" as passed away. Also of importance is the international health care debate, which relentlessly points to the United States ranking 37/191 countries in overall health system. But wait...as previously mentioned, the life expectancy measure is not what it seems to be and the World Health Report of 2000 used that factor as 25% of how to rank a country's health care system. Another 25% of the ranking came from "distribution of health" or fairness of receiving health care. As a result, 50% of the World's Health Report is completely false.

Where do we go from here? It is a dreadful and serious situation when the United States of America, who is the last great hope in healthcare, is going in the direction (rapidly) of socialized medicine. At the same time, those countries stuck with socialized medicine are realizing they have made a huge mistake! How can helpful change take place to improve healthcare in the United States?

5 Important steps to Health Care Reform

1. Make health care coverage portable.

This will end the problem of employees trying to remain in jobs they don't like. People won't be locked in just because they happen to have health insurance. Jobs are hard to come by these days and if someone has the opportunity to make that transition, health care should not keep them from moving. The average person has 5 -6 different occupations in their lifetime. Portability in this day and age is a practical solution.

2. Make Health Insurance tax-free

If individuals can purchase health insurance with tax-free dollars then individuals and families would be able to deduct health care premiums from their taxes. If companies are allowed to deduct the cost of coverage why can't individuals. 176 million people are enrolled in company -owned health plans. Tax-free health insurance might help to incentivize and correct this imbalance. Companies could compete to offer tax-free supplemental compensation, allowing employees to buy additional insurance, which would help those with pre-existing conditions.

3. Allow health insurance to be sold across state lines.

There is a huge discrepancy between states and insurance premiums. According to the preferred provider organization plan at www. ehealthinsurance.com a 25 yr old, non-smoking male in New Jersey pays out an unbelievable amount for the cheapest plan at a rate of over $3,000. Compare that against a state like Kentucky, which has less regulation than New Jersey. This male pays around $330 for the same coverage. That is quite a difference.

4. Tort reform

Tort reform must be a part of rebuilding our health care system. It's a crime that the Obama administration did not include this in their legislation. Instituting tort reform in the court system would give back to the healthcare system 54 billion dollars, as the average lawsuit is around $100,000 per case. What an incredible amount of money wasted over frivolous lawsuits. A lack of tort reform puts an unnecessary burden on our doctors and forces patients to partake in a larger amount of needless tests, driving costs up even more. Just think of the wasted time and energy a doctor must go through to deal with all the harassment that comes from overzealous lawyers looking to cash in. Also, malpractice insurance is becoming so expensive that young people are thinking twice about choosing medicine as a profession. Malpractice insurance can run some doctors around $250,000. I know it costs this much because one of my relatives business is medical malpractice insurance.

5. Vouchers are game changers.

A voucher system is a way to help the poor obtain insurance if they have no way of getting it. These vouchers are a much simpler solution compared to a bill that is filled with thousands of pages of regulation. The government would provide the poor with say, $5,000 in vouchers to buy health insurance that fits their needs.

Obamacare means a reduction in competition combined with government mandates. This includes males obtaining maternity care or substance abuse care as part of their coverage even if they have never used drugs. Obamacare states that you must pay for everything even if you don't want it. In the near future, Obamacare is set to limit the states that insurance companies can operate in; narrowing the range of choices consumers will have for their health insurance. This will ultimately cause many to drop their current coverage. There will also be increased discrimination against Health Savings Accounts, our most effective way to keep healthcare costs under control. Incentive will be switched from performing well, to just doing more even if that means lower quality of care. Hospitals will become crowded if, after all, everything is free.

Thanks to the leadership of people like Governor Mitch Daniels, the American people have a chance to fight back. Governor Daniels has implemented a far superior plan than the mess liberals and Obama have handed us. In Indiana, 5/6 all state employees and all members of the program for the uninsured have personal accounts that call for first dollar decisions. Meaning they must take responsibility for their medical choices. Money that they don't spend is theirs to keep, save and grow! They have seen a very big difference in cost once people take ownership and personal responsibility for their own healthcare. What a concept -allowing individuals to make their own decisions about what they want to buy. We must continue to put pressure on the Obama administration. The pushback against socialized medicine was working. Unfortunately, the deciding vote cast by conservative Chief Justice Roberts, ushered in the area of socialized medicine for America in June 2012. Our only hope is to elect presidential hopeful Mitt Romney to repeal this monstrosity before it costs us trillions and ruins the best healthcare system in the world.

E is for the "Economy"

We've had many Democratic Presidents in the past 100 years all following a similar pattern of thought: Centralized planning. From Wilson to Hoover to FDR to LBJ- the theme of big government has been used over and over. When uncovering their records on spending, taxation and regulation, it tells an eerily similar path. Hoover was an engineer, a planner, who favored the brainpower of the elite, hiked tariffs, government spending, tax increases and social programs. Hoover increased the deficit from 462 million in 1931 to 2.7 billion in 1932. He is called the grandfather of the new deal. FDR hammered Hoover on his liberal fiscal policies, which he then took to record levels. FDR inherited a debt of 22.5 billion and doubled it in 7 years. FDR's answers to the economic woes were deficit spending, increasing the national debt and fairness. Looking back on history reveals how these economic ideologies came to be the shared mantra for economic progress, according to liberals, with fairness centered at the core. The core idea that poverty is unfair and its government's job to redeem the individual by standing up for the poor and taking out the rich became the laborer v. the capitalist. The lure of profit portrayed individuals as being corrupt. FDR then went on to expand designs of Keynes economics as he promoted the concept of government intervention to secure a "bright future" for all. Like Keynes himself, FDR believed in spending oneself in prosperity as the "end all be all." He even fancied a 2nd bill of rights, which could have created a utopian society according to FDR. The new deal put into place collective bargaining and labor legislation on one side while restricting competition by creating a reduction in private corporate control.

Liberal presidents of the past all shared a common inept ability to see past their reckless spending, something our current administration knows all too well. It is imperative to remember that it is not just Obama who is at fault for spending far beyond our means, but the Democratic Party as well. Democrats might not call themselves socialist but that is exactly what they have become, a mere branch of Western Europe, whose very existence is consumed with equality over freedom. The liberal Democratic Party of the United States has based their mantra on spending for equality. They would rather spend trillions more than we have in order to promote equality even if it bankrupts the country. Their mindset is, it's ok to spend past our means, because "our intention was good." Liberal, socialist Democrats are speeding up the impending demise of this country faster than Usain Bolt running the 200m dash at the Olympics. The Obama administration is increasing our debt by four billion dollars every day! Put another way, $41,222/second!!! This reckless spending only leads to one direction -deflationary debt. When a country spends trillions more than it takes in, interest must be paid on the money that you borrowed. As time goes on, the government pays more and more interest until the only amount that can be paid is the interest. Eventually the country goes into bankruptcy and that is what we have become in America: 16 trillion dollars in debt. The picture looks much worse when considering unfounded liabilities that our government owes to the tune of 120 trillion dollars. Add that on top of the growing 16 trillion and we are looking at a whooping 136 trillion dollars or 10 times our GDP. We are collapsing from within and the only group that continually calls for fiscal responsibility - Tea Party Patriots! Obviously we must do all we can to combat radical terrorism, but liberal leaders are doing far more damage to this country by imposing their absurd idea of limitless spending. According to some estimates, the United States debt will be at 120% of GDP in 3-5 years, and that's not counting unfounded liabilities! 120% is the magic number at which countries can no longer service its debt and become bankrupt just like Greece. Yet liberals only call for more spending!

Economic reform cannot come soon enough. As it's said, if you don't learn from history, you are doomed to repeat it.

History can teach us a lesson

1933-1940 saw the doubling of federal spending from 4.6 billion to 9.5 billion mostly on domestic programs. Change came about in the form of government interference, as debt soared to new and disastrous heights. The role of nanny state supervision took over in 1946, as our national debt was nearly 122% of GNP. We can thank Democratic presidents for more than 390 new domestic social programs added during JFK and LBJ's administrations. They went from 45 –435 in just 8 years. Also, LBJ and his congress enacted 100s of new subsidies in welfare programs, housing programs, urban programs and education programs. Now we are left with Obama, who clearly shares the same idea of limitless spending of his liberal predecessors.

In the summer of 2011, Obama started comparing himself to Reagan. One could sense the desperation as he attempted to liken himself to one of the most popular presidents ever, while at the same time trying to show that he isn't so far left, despite his record indicating otherwise. Obama calls more press conferences to talk and talk about creating jobs except he never implements *action* towards real job creation. It is really quite amazing actually. He thinks that the more he talks about doing something the more something will just fall into place. I'm sorry but in the real world, action is required. In 1981 President Reagan helped create 20 million new jobs, on top of which he reduced inflation from 13.5 percent in 1980 to 4.1 percent by 1988, truly was an amazing achievement. Reagan's plans led to a reduction in unemployment from 7.6 percent to 5.5 percent. Other major triumphs included raising the real gross national product by 26 percent and cutting the prime interest rate by over half from 21.5 percent in 1981 to 10 percent in 1988. Another accomplishment was the increase in individual tax revenues, which rose from 244 billion in 1980 to 446 billion by 1989. Tax revenues grew by 99.4 percent throughout the 1980's and gave America 92 months of real economic growth. Reagan created such dramatic turnaround because of his belief in the individual and the reduction in government's role. His belief was to let each person make his way through life with hard work and less restraints holding him back. The freedom to pursue economic liberty was the calling card of his administration and they went to work by breaking down obstacles to personal freedom. For instance, President Reagan slashed marginal tax rates from 70 percent to 28 percent producing an enormous increase to the federal government. Revenues went from 500 billion to a ridiculous 1.1 trillion in 1990. Remember, he did this by lowering tax rates. What liberals need to understand is this; when taxes reach certain thresholds it becomes a deterrent for individuals and in the end reduces the amount of revenue the federal government collects. The laffer curve demonstrates this beautifully.

The Laffer Curve

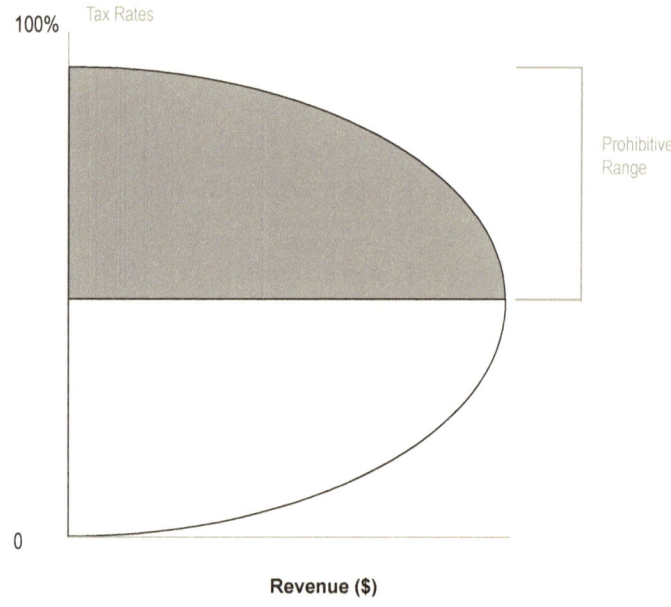

Source: Arthur B. Laffer

Another pro-economic, pro-growth move that Reagan implemented was to free workers from the stranglehold that Unions had over workers.

A present day opposing view comes from the Obama administration that is acting like a dictatorship by blocking the relocation of Boeing from Washington to South Carolina. South Carolina is a right –to-work state and Boeing should be able to open up a plant there if that is their wish. However, the National Labor Relations Board (NLRB) in an ultimate power grab, tried to prevent them from opening up this plant because they want to control their workers in every possible way, even if it means stopping Boeing from providing more jobs. If that isn't an assault on free market principles then I don't know what is. Thankfully, Boeing prevailed but not before a huge struggle with the Obama administration that is acting more like a dictatorship then a representative. The Obama administration is in deep trouble since the American people are out of jobs. Liberal congressmen are only left pandering to their leftist base while the American people watch jobs go by the wayside. Comically, Obama talks about being above partisan politics. I don't believe there has ever been a president as partisan as this one.

More spending, more taxes?

Has anything changed in terms of out control liberal spending? Well, not quite. Forty-eight months is all it took for this administration to add over 5 trillion dollars to our national debt. Let me repeat that>over 5 trillion dollars in 4 years. This number is basically the same as Bush's record amount of spending at 4.9 trillion dollars. Except Bush's 4.9 trillion happened in eight years not 4 years! Recall, those figures are according to the Treasury Department. The day Obama set foot into office we were looking at a debt of 10.62 trillion and now we sit over 16 trillion. Some might argue that America always increases its debt. Yes, but not this much, this quickly and for what? What have we gotten that is so wonderful from all this accumulation of debt? We have 8.2% unemployment (the real number is 15% unemployment because the CBO excludes those who want to work but have not searched in over 4 weeks along with part time workers who would like to work full time) only because the Congressional Budget Office counts unemployment figures in a false manner. What else have we received from the administration…out of control entitlement spending, and speeches, yes lots of speeches. We've also been provided with a decrease in security, increase in lawyers aiding terrorists at Guantanamo Bay, a monstrosity health care bill that the majority of the American public did not ask for, no true plan in Afghanistan or Pakistan, a stimulus plan that only put money into the pockets of Union leaders instead of the American people and a total lack of leadership on the part of Obama and the Democrats. It has been well over 1000 days since Obama and his team of czars have taken over the oval office and we still have not seen one clear-cut plan to jump-start this economy. Republicans had to take over Congress to even set the talks in motion. The election of 2010 was one of the most significant in history because it took absolute control out of the most radical administration the country has ever seen. The one and only answer he and the Democrats can give us is…taxes and more taxes on the rich.

We all can agree that the top 5% of taxpayers pay 59.6% of all income taxes. That's indisputable. What's also true is that those 5% earn 35% of all the income and yet are stuck with the majority of taxes. Taxing the rich *more* will not take care of our spending problem. What needs to change is the amount of spending we do each year and this is primarily the fault of the left. Revenue has not changed much, but the all out spending spree keeps going and going and going like the energizer bunny. This complete disregard for fiscal responsibility is sending us to the brink of bankruptcy. Comparing 2007 to 2011 isn't even a fair game. We took in 2.568 trillion in revenues and spent 2.728 trillion for a deficit of 160 billion. Not good, but not off the charts. In 2011 we were scheduled to take in 2.230 trillion and spend 3.629 trillion leaving us a deficit of 1.399 trillion dollars! That's an added debt of 1.239 trillion dollars, or another way to put it is that we had an added increase of just over 900 billion in spending but only 338 billion decreases in revenue. As we know Congress controls spending and not the president. Therefore, taking the 12 years of Congressional control that Republicans had during the Clinton and Bush years, the total amount added to the national debt was 3.873 trillion. This is far below what Democrats have added in only 1/3 that time! Democrats and Republicans really are different in the way in which they strive to accomplish their goals.

Truths, facts and fiction on socialism

There are many differences between Democrats and Republicans and perhaps none bigger than the two economic schools of thought in socialism v. capitalism. These two opposing sides take us in drastically different economic directions when it comes to how a society functions. Conservatives favor free markets while liberals favor government intrusion. As Winston Churchill so aptly put it, "The inherent vice of capitalism is the unequal sharing of blessings and the inherent vice of socialism is the equal sharing of miseries." As another great English leader so rightly stated, "the problem with socialism is that you eventually run out of other peoples' money to spend"- Margaret Thatcher.

Anyone reading this has to admit 2011 was chaotic. Whether it was the mayhem in the Middle East or riots and violence in Europe, to the United States on the verge of bankruptcy, to people marching in the streets, 2011 was pretty crazy. If you ask liberals why protests took place in Europe and American you will get a much different response when compared to conservatives. Liberals decry that the riots are taking place because of three main reasons. Entitlements are being taken away, unemployment is up and the rich are not being taxed enough. If the rich were taxed more, they could redistribute more of that money around to everyone else. You will get a far different response form conservatives. We don't feel there are too few entitlements but far too many! The nanny state has grown far too big, handed out too much money to those who are unwilling to work and the government can't afford it! The word of the year for 2011 was unsustainable. Governments are broken across the world and all the entitlement payments are unsustainable. Yet, all those people rioting in England and Greece aren't exactly poor. Nor are the unhappy people in America. Take for example the average per capita GDP. In the United States it's at $47,000 and reaches $35,000 in England. If these rioters are so poor then why are they bent on stealing smart phones, Nikes, and flat screen televisions? You have to pay monthly fees for technology items. Cable isn't free. The obsession with material goods is one reason for the riots. We are told we can't be happy without these things. We are also told that we have the world at our fingertips, if we only purchase that sweet new cell phone. This we know is baloney. People have only had smart phones for a few years now and we've done just fine without them. The real problem is government wiping your nose at every level, as this does far more damage than anything else. Government's role should be limited enabling freedom to flourish for each individual. Of course some people need help and they can get that help from a variety of places. Shelters and church -sponsored charities are wonderful at getting people back on their feet and moving in the right direction. Why should our government be writing checks to more than 45 million people when our government is broken? The behemoth that is the entitlement sector of America and Europe is breaking down. People get upset when goodies are taken away. We are witnessing this effect in an eye opening fashion.

Government doesn't create money it spends money!

Socialism is probably the least understood political system despite its grip on so many billions of people around the world. Who has the power in this form of government? Who controls whom? Does it make income equal? We must figure out what socialism really is, because after all, Democrats are the party of socialism.

Socialism dramatically increases government spending and adds tremendously to the debt. Massive debt results in the death of an economy and gets the ball rolling for the death of a country. Socialism siphons wealth and productivity from private sector and puts it in the hands of the central planners. Yet, the most important factor to remember about socialism is not so much the redistribution of wealth, but the redistribution of power from the people to the central planners. When socialism becomes your economic preference, you the people, have no choice but to do what the government tells you to do. You become a puppet. Freedom to live, as you want to live, disappears along with your drive to succeed and the ability to provide for your family. Government intrusion undermines personal responsibility, and at the same time reduces incentives to work and save.

It insulates people and business from consequences of bad decisions. So why is there one single person in the United States that still believes in this freedom- sucking system of rule? The immediate reaction from liberals has been two- fold. They simply think everything will be equal and therefore a utopia. Or they insist on saying that the right kind of socialism has never been implemented. However, when has the "right kind" ever been employed? If I could give you an example of a purely socialist country that has succeeded I would share it with you.

Socialism is much more than redistribution of wealth through taxes and government assistance programs. It's a system of central planning. This is important to remember. Why would anyone endorse a system that gives such great authority to a tiny amount of "chosen" people? Think about it, you are giving up your freedom when subscribing to socialism. You are saying to a few powerful men in government: plan everything! Tell me when and where I can build my house, even though I won't fully own it. Tell me at what prices I can buy fruit. Provide state schooling, even if the schooling is not particularly good. The obvious answer here is risk aversion. Those who are scared are in favor of socialism. Risk adverse people want life taken care of for them. Even if it means truly giving up their freedom. People who support socialism will not become entrepreneurs nor will they go off to start their own business. They want security. Liberals would rather have a government-run healthcare system that is inefficient, lacks innovation and has inferior quality in exchange for the simple fact that it is in place. The other lightening quick synopsis of socialism is the absence of prices. A particular product or service has a different value and certain worth to each person, at different times, in a certain context, in juxtaposition with other goods and services. That is why socialism loves to piggyback off price levels set in the free market, otherwise socialistic countries would be in even worse shape. Although socialism continually aims to break from a price-based economy with prices set by government officials, it's impossible to do so and has never been successfully accomplished throughout history.

Does the slippery slope apply to socialism? One can easily make the argument that socialism and Communism are basically one in the same. Some countries remain under the rule of totalitarian rule (North Korea,

Cuba, and Venezuela), a more hardcore form of socialism/communism, while other countries prefer partial democratic/socialism mix like Sweden and India. A quarrelsome sore spot for supporters of socialism is their constant attempt at distancing themselves from communism. The key point is that they are both Marxist. In the words of Harvard professor Sweezy, the founder of *Monthly Review,* the leading socialist journal in the United States had this to say: "Socialism and communism are alike in that both are systems of production for use are based on public ownership of the means of production and centralized planning. Socialism grows directly out of capitalism; it is the first form of the new society. Communism is a further development or "higher stage" of socialism." As Kevin Williamson writes in his book, *The Politically Incorrect Guide to Socialism,* "The difference between the two is tactical and technical." In order to change the nature of the state, a classless society must be implemented. Socialism on the other hand believes that the nature of the state can remain in some form but it's just a matter of who can obtain control of said state. Use the given framework at hand but simply keep hammering away at it until you achieve the infusion of socialism. Socialism will then use central planning, or the state, as its means of production for the citizen (supposedly outsmarting trillions upon trillions of calculations per second) providing the perfect amount of every product and service for each individual. Yet, that is simple impossible. Williamson sums it up beautifully, "when it comes to the deep structural issues in the economy – investment, infrastructure, large-scale property rights, capital markets, trade, etc – socialism and communism are in the words of America's leading socialist thinkers – identical." "This doesn't mean that we should expect Sweden to be as repressive and backwards as the Soviet Union was; it means we should expect Sweden under socialism to very much resemble Sweden under communism." This is so well put, but yet this kind of thinking does not reach any media outlets. It is this kind of common sense; logical, forthright thinking that spells things out very clearly.

Believers in socialism do so because they think what a wonderful concept it is for everyone to have less and instead, just rely on the state to take care of you. What people fail to comprehend is that you ultimately become a pawn. You have no choice but to go along with what government tells you to do. You have less freedom, less options, less independence. On top of which: you become poor along with everyone else you know, while a few powerful people keep all the money and direct the people and money as they see fit. Socialism doesn't spread the wealth; it spreads massive poverty. Socialism is a failed economic experiment that eventually runs out of money resulting in the deaths of millions through starvation, torture and corruption. If you do not value your freedom nor your prosperity then sign up for socialism, always remembering that it is basically the same political scheme as communism. If you want independence, and the ability to live as free as you possibly can, then embrace capitalism. Inevitably, the conflict between socialism and capitalism comes back to selfishness. Strident socialists carry the belief that removing the selfish nature of humans will lead to a utopian society where wealth is continually spread equally among the people. However, you should never view capitalism as a selfish form of business. Instead view capitalism as a form of "rational self-interest." Selfishness implies gaining something at the expense of others. Rational self-interest means interactions with others for the benefit of all, in a free market where one produces, buys and sells products and services that are exchanged voluntarily. Capitalism is to the benefit of all, as opposed to socialism, which benefits only a tiny fraction of people: those in government.

What government does well is spend your money. When politicians fail, they fail with your money. Their solution: to spend more money to fix the problem, then proceed to applaud themselves for spending all your hard-earned money. Politicians like telling us what we should do and how they will implement their plan. Take high-speed rail for instance. It is a nice idea in theory, but in reality it doesn't work. No one rides the train, its heavily subsidized by the government, it costs too much to construct and people like using their cars. The problem is, once you trust the government to provide for the people, you derail innovation. There is more incentive to just get by and do what you've always done, then to respond to changing tastes from consumers. Just look at how Silicon Valley emerged. No interference from politicians, no buearocrats, no central planners, no academics, no groups of people sitting around a desk trying to plan it. The marvel of Silicon Valley's materializing happened because of private entrepreneurship responding to market opportunity. If the owners got it wrong they lost their shirt. If politicians get it wrong, we the people lose our shirt.

The private sector on the other hand gives us a much better product at a lower price because there is competition! What happens in the free market is called spontaneous order. This great concept does something special. It leaves people alone and allows entrepreneurs to create and see the needs and desires of society to satisfy their well- being. People respond to the markets signals, the biggest one being prices. Prices tell producers what is needed, how urgently and where to put it. Market prices are infinitely more productive than relying on a handful of central planners (the elites) who pretend to know what is good for society when they don't have a clue. The elites went to Ivy League schools and are very book smart. Yet they will never be smarter than market forces. The elites feel they are smarter than you or I and this somehow justifies their attempts at manipulating the market because they are doing it for the "good" of the economy. Well it never ends up that way. Central planners believe they can predict the future and but since they are playing with the taxpayers money it really doesn't matter to them if they screw things up. As we've seen since getting off the gold standard in 71', they'll just print more money. In reality politicians are just starting to make money for the first time in their lives, as government workers. Even if they were geniuses, government officials couldn't possibly predict all the infinite bits of information needed to make things work in combination with millions of people all at the same time. Information and needs are interspersed throughout the economy and brought together by the forces of supply and demand with changes in prices. Politicians have never been able to account for all the variables in the history of mankind. Despite the track record of 0% success rate, it hasn't keep governments from trying. They keep trying because they believe they are smarter then the rest of us. When central planners control the economy, they control the people. Just look at the former Soviet Union. They are infamous for long lines of people looking for toilet paper. Oranges and bananas were rare commodities. The leading causes of fires were due to explosions of Soviet made televisions. The leaders made sure that the people got televisions (presumable to continue their indoctrination of government propaganda), they also had television czars and a government factory to produce this terrible product, using smart people to run it. The results were fewer televisions produced and more televisions that exploded. If it were left to free interaction among many different people working together, they would have produced a much higher quality at a much lower price.

As renowned historian Niall Ferguson explains in his book, Civilization, "The planned economy mobilized manpower to work on heavy industry, infrastructure and arms; and it financed the process through forced savings. As a result, consumption stagnated. People worked and got paid, but because there was steadily less and less to buy in the shops, they had little option but to put the money in savings accounts, where it was recycled into funding the government." In other words, the surest way to destroy a society is to allow for the implementation of a planned economy.

It comes down to another war of ideology. The invisible hand of capitalism works. The self-interest of every human being allows for stability. When things get out of whack the invisible hand of the markets has a way of correcting life through what people want and their drive to fulfill their needs. It just works. The majority of our economy is an example of spontaneous order. Shelves are usually full with all kinds of products that we need and want. There are usually just enough of them as well. Not too many, not too few. The invisible hand truly is amazing. The power of pricing sends signals to either make more or consider using scarce resources in a different way. These signals send indications to the American people far better than government elites could ever hope to. It is government's involvement in the economy that screws things up. In summary, get out of our way!

Perhaps nothing better illustrates just how incredible the free market is than the pencil. Despite the chaos that takes place every day in the market, products gets produced by many individuals each playing their part while getting paid accordingly. Read the brilliant essay "I Pencil", by Leonard E. Read from 1958." When reading his most famous essay, it shows how producing something as simple as a pencil takes on a whole new light once you see the dynamics of free market principles. In fact I really feel that liberals should read the essay because they are the ones that are truly overwhelmed in life. I believe they have long since resigned to the fact that if life is too hard for them, it must be too hard for others less fortunate. Consequently someone or something larger must step up to make decisions, provide help and steer them in the right direction. While we are at it, pay for benefits as well! As a result, liberals enlist the help of the government. I am not saying people don't deserve help, because some people really do need assistance, in particular the mentally ill and those who become physically impaired. What I am pointing out is that life is different for everyone across the board. We all strive to make the best life possible for ourselves, enjoy the time we have on earth and to help others when we can. However, the implementation of socialism does not allow for this. Life becomes miserable for all. You lose your freedom and you become herded cattle taking your place in line for the "betterment of the government." Socialism is sickening to think about and in the end, only leads ones country down the path of self-destruction.

The great big lie of capitalism is that it's a zero sum game. As it is said, a rising tide lifts all boats. Just because businessman "A" becomes rich does not mean that average Joe "B" becomes less average. Nor does it mean that average Joe has less money. In fact, just the opposite has been shown to be true. There is no finite amount of money out there. Liberals always confuse success for one as a loss for another. This is simply not true. If businessman "A" makes a large sum of money, he is able to hire people at his company. He can provide health benefits and a steady income to those who are hired. Historical examples are abundant when looking at countries in the past. Accumulation of wealth showed that not only did the rich get richer but the poor became wealthier as well. This happened in Italy in the 1400s, Britain in the 1800s, United States in the 1900s along with India and China as well. Look at what happened between 1998 and 2007. This was a period in which over 1,000 people every day moved from the 9 states with the highest income tax to the 9 states with no income tax. During this time the states with no income tax created 89% more jobs and saw a

32% increase in personal income than tax heavy states. The heavily taxed states (not surprisingly included California, New York, New Jersey) had or continue to have liberal state governments whose intention is to punish those "greedy" rich people. Thankfully we have 50 states and not all of them are filled with liberal state governments. Even those who inherit huge sums of money end up helping the less fortunate. The rich invest money and production into society along with the consumption of goods. In the interest of self-preservation, the invisible hand works.

Democrats: Big government, Keynesian economics, central planning, higher taxes, heavy regulation, political power>control over others, redistribute wealth, nanny state = socialism

Republicans: Limited government intrusion, free markets decides, invisible hand, less regulation, money power>control over oneself, lower taxes, reducing the debt = capitalism

Government manipulation of the books, Clinton v. Bush

Almost every time an argument comes up between democrats and republicans as to why the economy is in such a mess, historical inaccuracies are usually mentioned in regards to Clinton and Bush. Liberals put out the same argument that Clinton left with a surplus and Bush left us with debt. That must mean big government is better at spending our money than we are and that tax breaks "for the rich" are a horrible idea. These two themes don't add up when we take a closer look. When Democrats say it is ok to spend more than what you take in, common sense leads you to believe that deficit spending is inevitable. My father always said that in sports, "there is no substitute for speed." In politics; there is no substitute for cooking the books, especially when the public doesn't know.

When the CBO reported that Clinton ran surpluses from 1998 –2001, it was the first surplus in 28 years. Very impressive Bill, or was it? Hmmm. How could a guy who believes in big government spending;

cradle to the grave economics, heavy regulation and central planning run a surplus? Since our national debt rose every single year under Clinton how could it be possible to leave a surplus? Play with the numbers enough and you'll get whatever you want. Using 2009 dollars, his debt started at 6.2 trillion when he came into office in 1992 and it ended around 7 trillion, eight years later. A 13% increase isn't bad compared to some but it is still 800 billion. What happened? It is all in the way the government calculates its numbers. The way in which government began calculating its debt started with Reagan, so it's not just a Democratic tactic. Nevertheless, millions still sight facts supporting big government liberal spending because Clinton had a surplus. It is simply not true. Since our government intentionally makes this complicated forcing people to waste valuable time arguing over these discrepancies, let us just get to the most important part: balancing of our national debt. A real cash surplus means our national debt goes down. If we have a cash deficit then our national debt goes up and we have to borrow more money leading to deficit spending. Clinton boasted that he had the largest one-year debt reduction, 223 billion in one year and 360 billion in 3 years. CNN gave number sighting the federal budget surplus for fiscal year 1999 was 122.7 billion and 69.2 billion for fiscal year 1998. This, they insisted, lead the Treasury to pay down 138 billion in national debt. But it's just not true. Look at the record, according to the House Office of Management and Budget. Clinton inherited a national debt of about 4 trillion in 1993 at $4,351,000,000,000. Upon leaving office in Sept 2000 he left the US with national debt number of $5,605,000,000,000. If he arrived at 4.3 and left at 5.6, a surplus is mathematically impossible. It is a bit sad that we even have to go over this but this is D.C. politics and it's played everyday. The game is played by changing data and breaking government debt into two categories instead of one and only reporting one category. There is public debt (what we owe to bondholders) and intergovernmental debt- what we owe to ourselves. When we put these 2 together we arrive at our true national debt. However, former President Clinton chose to only use on the public debt and chose to ignore the intergovernmental debt. That is very convenient, since this part of the debt goes up every year. All he did was borrow every dollar of the trust and count it as new income to spend instead of debt. This ridiculous form of "income" offset all the other debt he was running up. To make it simpler: a guy makes $50,000 at his job and spends $54,000. His uncle gives him $10,000 that he will have to repay in the future. Only a logical person will come to the conclusion that you now have personal debt of $10,000 and not a surplus of $4,000! Somehow our politicians have the nerve to count that as a $4,000 dollar surplus. This is just one reason why the American people want more transparency from our D.C. politicians.

Too much spending! Keynesians economics doesn't work

What does Keynesian economics really mean? After all, it is the central theme of the Democrats economic plan. It simply means this: spend yourself into wealth. Or another way to put it: the spending of a countries currency at will. This is why getting off Bretton Woods was such a big deal. Our currency (now) is tied to nothing and therefore it can be printed at will, without repercussion…until it's too late. (Remember Obama borrowed more in the month of February 2011 alone (223 billion) than George Bush did during the entire 2007 budgetary year (163 billion)). The real test to figuring out whether or not there is a Keynesian agenda is really pretty simple. Does the government have power over the money supply? Remember believers in the Keynesian system thought all that America needed to get out of the Great Depression was to pump more money into the economy. Somehow, it was just a matter of being, "too little too late." This economic stance still resonates with liberals today, who feel that more spending continues to be the answer. We have seen this fall short in the form of Obama's failed stimulus plan. Democrats' economic plans have not worked in the past; they are not working today and will not work in the future. The only thing pumping more money into the economy did was delay the Great Depression by about 15 years. Relentless money printing inevitably leads to rising prices because there are too many dollars chasing too few goods.

A perfect example of government's interference was the excessive printing of the money supply that eventually led to the economic crisis in 2000. Then fed chairman, Alan Greenspan slashed interest rates and enacted huge government spending to allow for government conjecture. At first this interference of low interest helped provide corrections in the market but did not lead to any huge economic recovery. Conversely, in doing so he created another bubble that was far bigger than the internet one. The real estate bubble will go down as the largest one in history (so far). Fast forward to 2010 and you can see that, indeed, central bankers and their theory of pumping money has given us a sever recession. The crashing of mortgage giants has been a major threat to our entire financial situation as a whole. The creation of the two mortgage giants Fannie Mae and Freddie Mac who underwrote 80% of the mortgage credit in 2007 are bankrupt. These two nationalized banks took on huge risks, took out private banks and helped create the largest debt bubble ever. The United States government bailed out those institutions with the government rescue package making them total property of the United States government, leaving the losses on the doorstep of every United States taxpayer. Democrats and central bankers really helped fuel the fire for global debt.

Democrats like to spend money and when the government uses domestic savings to finance expenditures it forces competition with the credit needs of private enterprises. Therefore interest rates have nowhere to go but up because the implementation of money is given the opposite effect. When money printing gets out of control there is a very popular way to get out of it – inflation. Inflation transfers the burden to the American people and in doing so, reduces wealth. It is a very sneaky way of politicians to say, "Look at all that we have provided for you." The problem with this scenario is that companies have been making the public share in their losses during difficult times but have not shared in times of profit. This has lead to the backlash against banks across America.

The Keynesian theory of economics continues to remain popular, in particular with Democrats, only because liberal politicians relentlessly promote it. It's a perfect setup for self-serving politicians because it provides them with the opportunity to spend money on goodies for their constituents and in turn buy votes. If the people who provide votes want handouts, then it's up to elected official to get them. The politicians don't care because it's all about the here and now. It doesn't matter to them if they hurt the American people in the long run. The politicians only care about staying in power and do so by promoting Keynesian spending by handing out goodies.

What if we had a real world example of Keynesian economics failing to work? I am not talking about Obama's failed stimulus, which we will come to in a moment. I am speaking of the misquoted notion of World War II government spending saving our economy. According to respected writer, Arthur Herman of *The Ultimate Stimulus,* World War II caused our government to borrow some 30 TRILLION dollars (in today's money). Keynesians argue that this is what turned the economy around during the time of WWII. Somehow borrowing trillions dropped unemployment 9.5% to 1.2% and ended the Great Depression. However, upon review from leading economist Robert J. Barro, the solution to our economic woes certainly was not through deficit spending (nor is it today). As Barro explains, "The data showed that output expanded during World War II by less than the increase in military purchases." Private consumption, investments and net exports actually fell because resources were needed for military production. In reality, World War II government spending was responsible for halting growth in the private sector. Clear evidence points to an economic rebound before the United States jumped into the war. As Arthur Herman pointed out, "GNP jumped from 90.5 billion in 1939 to 124.5 billion just before the Pearl Harbor attacks, when government spending was still at relatively low levels." "Then with mobilization, private consumption and investment slowed and headed south – while government deficit spending headed sharply north, rising from 6 billion in 1940 to 89 billion in 1944." Proponents of large deficit spending argued that wartime spending increases were what got things moving in the right direction because the unemployment numbers plummeted. As Lee Corso, from ESPN's College Football's Gameday says, "Not so fast my friend!" Remember 16 million men were pulled out of the labor market and into the military to defend our nation. That is a reduction of 22% of our labor force, meaning unemployment had nowhere to go but down. When World War II ended, military spending had no where to go but down, collapsing from 37.5% of GDP in 1945 to 5.5% of GDP in 1947. Keynesians thought this would create wide scale unemployment and called on the government action to alleviate desperate times ahead. But the Keynesians were wrong! Large unemployment did not occur. The United States economy grew from 231 billion GDP in 1947 and jumped to 285 billion by 1950. There remain facts that ca not be explained away by feelings and wishes. The end of World War II did not result in fallout of savings. Research shows that in fact, the opposite was true as peoples liquid assets continued to grow from 151 billion at the end of 1945 to 168.5 billion at the start of 1948. Therefore, stimulation of the economy was not created by people unloading their savings accounts, but rather by a quick rise in private capital investments. The New Deal had slowed down private investments and when the war hit it really stopped people from investing. Herman showed that, "that when the war ended, investments jumped from 10.6 billion in 1945 to **46 billion** in 1948 as plants expanded and retooled for the production of civilian goods." Private investments increased as a percentage from 5 percent to 18 percent and this allowed for more growth and hiring. Did anything else spur growth instead of government stimulus? Yes indeed. Washington cut taxes! Respected writer Herman also showed that, "The Revenue Act of 1945 cut the top marginal tax rate from 94 percent to 86.4 percent, and the lowest marginal rate from 23 percent to 19 percent." Other important cuts included reducing the corporate tax rate and eliminating FDR's wartime price controls. We can take a guess at what happened next -revenues soared and the American economy was back on its way. For the next 20 years the GNP grew at a beautiful and steady rate of 4%. So much for the entire Keynesian (Liberal) economic theory…facts get in the way.

In the end, the keys to a healthy American economy- employment and increased wealth were no secret at all. Additionally, our situation isn't all that different from what we face today. Private investments, renewed confidence in business, reduced regulation and Republicans in charge are exactly what America needs today just as it did in the 1940s. Remember this sentence: Keynesians believe that you can somehow spend yourself into wealth. This economic belief does not make sense and never will – no matter how much money you throw at it. The shovel- ready projects will never be shovel ready. The biggest threat to individual freedom comes from the strongest organization of all…big government

Another great example at the hands of Keynesian economic failure is our present day situation given to us by liberals. We all know we can't keep spending at the rate that we are right now. We cannot allow ourselves to be fooled by sneaky, dubious politicians. We have recent proof that a nation cannot spend itself into prosperity. Thank you dictator Obama for providing us this proof. Obama stated in august of 2009 those who questioned his move for 800 billion-stimulus plan as "Phony arguments and petty politics." Obama also stated that he has "Rescued our economy from catastrophe." Unemployment stood at 9.4% and today it stands at 8.2% (with *true* unemployment at 15%). Keep in mind those who have believed in Obama and Democrats…he promised his steroid-spending plan would prevent unemployment from ever exceeding 8.0%. The unemployment number becomes much worse when you count all the people that are truly not in the labor force and we are left with 88 million people! Remember hope and change…Obama said his plan would save or create 3.5 million jobs. Government jobs are the only areas that have shown increases in employment. We are experiencing the change at the tune of a 50% increase in our national debt in 2 years! The national debt has increased 5 trillion dollars in 2 years and government spending as a percentage of GDP has increased by 25%. We are borrowing over 40 cents to every dollar we are spending. At the end of 2011 the total debt will equal the nation's entire economic output. Yes, you can even *hear* the real change from Obama and the economic belief system from liberals. That sound is your hard earned money being flushed down the toilet.

The big 3 loom over the US economy: Medicare, Medicaid and Social Security

By 2050 the cost of these 3 entitlements alone will increase from 8.4 of GDP to 18.6% of GDP. To cover these costs Congress would have to raise taxes on every household by over $12,000. To pay for all these promised funds the top tax would need to go from 35% to 77% and the 25% rate would need to hit 55%. Seventy-seven million baby boomers are starting to collect their Social Security, Medicare and Medicaid payments with retirees spending 1/3 of their adult lives in taxpayer-funded retirement. Meanwhile national security, education, health research and anti poverty programs are left fighting over the remaining scraps.

Medicare, Medicaid and Social Security already absorb 42% of federal budget and they are growing at 7% annually. Although, economic growth is one part of the solution it isn't *the* solution to alleviate our enormous burden from the big 3 since increased wages also imply increased social security benefits as those benefits are tied to wages. The factors that increase tax revenues also increase spending, leading to a 0 net gain in problem solving for the out of control costs these entitlement programs produce. Obviously eliminating waste is a must, but that does not completely solve the problem. Tax cuts are not enough either. If we let the 2001 and 2003 tax cuts expire, this would only provide a small increase in revenues - 23.4% by 2050. The problem is too much spending. We must not let ours focus get sidetracked by political gamesmanship. America has too many takers and not enough givers! In Reagan's last year in office, 1988, there was 400 billion in entitlement spending. As of 2010 we are now at 2 trillion! That doesn't even include food stamps. We are simply spending too much money on too many programs that only hand out money and don't take any in.

Social Security cost: 743 Billion

When it comes down to it, social security is a socialized government program that has never been properly administered. For those currently receiving benefits, they should continue to do so. However, at some point a cutoff must be made. I personally do not agree with the concept to begin with and wish it were never set up in the first place. It is basically a ponzi scheme aimed at helping the government collect more of your hard earned money. Americans have entrusted their hard-earned savings to our government and politicians who have raided that money as if it were revenue! The government is now making these payments of social security as IOUs. In short- the government no longer has the money to cover these debts. Our government is bankrupt. The American people shouldn't be forced to pay into something that they may never see in the future. Social Security puts more money into the hand of government fat cats. SinceSince, we know Democrats do not want to touch this with a 10-foot pole, the burden falls onto the Republican Party to make things happen. Social security, after all, is at the heart of what Democrats are all about> entitlements! Democrats act like little children who want full entitlements, increasing benefits and to never worry about paying for it. Republicans act like the responsible parents who have to tell the children, no! In fact we will be cutting back, because we can't afford this any longer. Clearly we need reform and it's going to come down to cutting benefits, which is something no one wants to hear but must accept. We can't continue on the current path we are on. Currently, America's social security system pays only 42 million Americans. However, this program will soon be responsible for 77 million, as baby boomers begin to retire in droves. Not only are more people being added to the plan but human beings are living longer as well. In 1940, a 65-year-old person could expect to live 13 years more. Now they live 18 years longer and that number is expanding to 22 years. Social security depends on having enough workers because it is based on payroll taxes. In 1960, five workers supported each retiree. This ratio has drop to 3:1 and will be 2:1 by 2030.

Medicare cost: 549 Billion

Promises have been made to millions of people and these promises are unsustainable. Government entitlements make people more resentful, helpless and eventually explodes into violence when the government has to take away some of the goodies that were promised. A perfect example would be the explosion that took place in London when unsustainable promises led to resentful rioters. The streets were filled with ungrateful people, looting beautiful old stores, stealing from their neighbor, burning buildings, beating people up in the street in the name of getting what they want. They are trying to justify their horrible acts by saying it's the rich who are at fault. In reality, the blame falls squarely on the shoulders of big government, since it is the government who is responsible for giving away billions in entitlements until it's no longer economically feasible. Responsibly, the labor party was removed in England and common sense has been restored to our proper cousins on the other side of the pond. The conservative party led by Prime Minister Cameron had to come in and clean up the mess. As Tim Montgomerie wrote in the Daily Telegraph in an October 2011 article: "Over the last week we has seen the culmination of the liberal experiment and it doesn't work. The liberal experiment that two parents don't matter, welfare rather than work cures poverty, tolerate moderate crime, turn a blind eye to celebrity drug use, allow children to leave school with out any worthwhile skills and that there's no difference between right and wrong. Now we've seen the results—Londoners rioting." It is becoming more and more apparent that liberals truly are the party of spoiled little children. The United States can't fall into the way of Europe, as liberals would so willingly love to have happen. We can't let liberals bleed us dry and fall into the hands of limitless entitlements. Part of what makes America great, what makes America exceptional, is that we have not gone the way of Europe. We must continue to fight so that we do not spend ourselves into oblivion with no way out. Deficit spending results in crippling debt and is what coincides with the end of a great nation. As is the case with Medicare, which is going broke and in less than 9 years this program will be bankrupt. Republicans put forth a plan to save Medicare and Democrats gave us…crickets. Medicare is chock full of runaway costs. The program is unsustainable and everyone can at least agree on that, yet the left and the right have very different views on how to fix this.

Things are not as they used to be. For instance, the average household spends 50 times more than they did on healthcare than in 1960. In the 60's we used to spend 5.6% of our economy on healthcare. That has now risen to 17.6%, a major difference. Currently we have 10,000 baby boomers being added to Medicare everyday! We can choose to do nothing and this socialized program will run out in 9-10 years, creating quite a problem for our seniors. Currently, 35 million people receive fee for service insurance plans. American seniors will see the price tag will double over the next 10 years, going from 526 billion to 980 billion. The system is set up for failure because it only allows for cost increases and ultimately leads to quality decreases, by having the patient visit the doctor for a service and that doctor in turn sends the bill to Medicare, who then pays the doctor for services rendered regardless of the quality of care. All this with our tax dollars and borrowed money! There is no financial incentive for doctors to delivery quality of care at an affordable price. Democrats' proposal has and continues to be: Let a panel of unelected, unaccountable bueaurocrats come in and decide how much or how little Medicare can pay that doctor. They also get to decide which services Medicare will or will not pay for. This is just another form of price control. This liberal method only encourages more consumption and as a side bonus forces doctors to bill non-Medicare patients more in the long run. In the future doctors will simply stop seeing Medicare patients. What doctor is going to want to be told how much they can charge and what services they can provide? This isn't Russia? It is actually a smooth transition to socialized medicine. Boards telling patients, "Oh we'll let you have the procedure this time but you've used up your x-ray this year, we won't allow it next time. Or, nope, sorry can't help you with that transplant; you're too old for us to waste a costly procedure on you." Thanks but no thanks. The American people do not want groups of 15 people sitting around a desk deciding whether or not my parents get the medical help or operation they may need. Talk about being two faced. Democrats accuse Republicans of hurting seniors while they are cutting 500 billion out of Medicare and creating panels to decide whether or not you can receive a service. Instead of pushing granny off the cliff, the Democratic Party is happily driving busloads of seniors off a mountain. Medicare's obvious problem is too much spending but it also lacks any sort of competition and innovation. Competition and innovation are the only solutions that are capable of turning around this out of control bus. Today's fee for service program simply doesn't work and at the same time crushes competition. Medicare pays the doctors and hospitals the same price for a specified service regardless of quality or efficiency. So whether the patient is happy or not with the outcome the same fee will apply. That creates a major problem because incentives are lost to reduce prices. Providers have no incentives to reduce costs because they will be paid the same no matter what. Efficiency is then lost and volume is increased. In the end health care costs have nowhere to go but up. When the individual has no say in the matter and the control rests in the hands of the central planners, hazards our inevitable. Our seniors have no say in the cost of Medicare, nor do they realize just how much healthcare costs. We need a better solution and premium support subsidies give Medicare a fighting chance.

Premium support subsidy would support each senior when choosing a private health insurer of his or her liking. Private insurers would be required to provide the same minimal level of coverage as Medicare currently does, but the individual would decide any coverage beyond this. If a senior wanted to go with an insurance company that was paying less, (than the premium supported payment provided by Medicare) then they would be free to do so and keep the difference. Conversely, if he or she chose a plan that was more than the premium supported payment of Medicare, than they would make up the difference with their own money. It is a good solution and frankly the only one. Seniors would still have a subsidized and guaranteed health plan but a lower cost because incentives have changed for both the consumer and the provider. It could help rein in the soaring costs and make the program more manageable. This plan also addresses the certain problem of the poor versus wealthy issue. Those with the least amount of money along with those with the worst health problems would receive greater support while the wealthiest would receive a smaller amount of help and use more of their own money.

A key point in the premium support plan is to know that it would grow at the current rate of inflation. This is good thing but some will argue that it leaves a problem left behind that we will get to a little later. The important point is this- it applies pressure and therefore helps to keep insurance costs down. Furthermore, it would help keep the programs growth rate in check. The numbers reveal a staggering amount of help. Ten years after implementation, the federal government would spend about 240 billion less per year on Medicare and after those first 10 years the cost of Medicare would actually decline as a share of GDP. By 2040 the CBO shows a savings of 900 billion per year! Now that is progress. The opposition to the premium support plan, in particular, is the fear that it wouldn't keep up with the insurance, resulting in more out of pocket costs for seniors. What this liberal view doesn't factor in is competition! Liberals don't even acknowledge that it could make a difference. Even if insurance costs outpace inflation there is nothing written in this plan saying it can't be reevaluated and adjusted accordingly. I am not saying it's the greatest plan out there but what else is there? I find it refreshing to see Republicans taking a stand on this issue and actually putting forth a plan to get America back on track. My only concern is the American people being fooled into thinking Liberals have come up with anything to help; because they haven't come up with anything at all. Only those who love moments of awkward silence would dare ask a liberal what they have proposed to save Medicare. More crickets…the national debt is expected to be twice as large as our economy in 2030 with Medicare playing the largest role. As our population gets older and older we will see the flawed design of Medicare take an even larger chunk of our debt problem with it. We must fundamentally alter the way Medicare works. The alternative is that it completely ends. In effect there really is no choice but to change Medicare. The only question remains, will Medicare be saved?

Medicaid cost: 240 Billion

It is safe to say there is a problem with Medicaid because it is broke, full of fraud, waste and needs reform. Medicaid was never intended to support people living this long. This program has been overextended and its time for a change. We need to give our states greater flexibility and deliver innovation. The goal is to provide service to those who need it most, but with an increase in responsibility while reducing cost so that it can continue. Without reducing costs, this program becomes unsustainable as well.

Up until 1965 health care for low-income people was strictly a state issue with barely any federal involvement. Things changed with the passage of Title XIX of the Social Security Act of 1965. A "partnership" was created between the states and federal government setting Medicaid on the wrong track every since. Although states were allowed to administer their own programs, the federal government set requirements for service delivery, quality and eligibility standards. In order to determine funding levels the Social Security Act of 1965 outlined Federal Medical Assistance Percentages (FMAP) to calculate federal government's financial contributions to each states specific program. In the 45 years since its inception, Medicaid has become an unaffordable burden on the American government. By 2019, state expenditures are projected to be $327.6 billion. It will be increasing at a compounding rate of 9.8%. Remember this is just Medicaid. We aren't talking about social security or Medicare. Nor are we discussing any other entitlement programs out there. Just Medicaid! By 2012 more than 45 states and the District of Columbia are expected to have budget shortfalls, exhorting further financial pressure. Combined with the fact that 69.5 million Americans are enrolled in Medicaid, or 1/5 in 2011 with an additional 25.6 million people being added in the coming decade adding 12 billion more to state debt with administration costs. Compounding this dilemma is that fact that doctors are increasingly skeptical to provide service to these people. A nationwide survey in June 2010, found 54.5% of primary care physicians are no longer accepting new Medicaid patients. It is a tough call for docs, because these patients generally require a lot more care. Also, doctors make less money each time they provide services for them. It becomes half charity work.

These three monstrous entitlement programs have left us with three tough choices if nothing is changed:

1. Massive tax increases that will choke off economic growth
2. Eliminate other federal programs all together
3. Budget deficits so high, we default on our debt

It's hard to deal with programs that grow each year but are never asked to reign in there spending habits. Eventually they have to be dealt with and it leads to tough decisions. Each year Congress basically just accepts the fact that 53% will be spent on entitlements and 9% will be spent for net interest. The rest is up for grabs among national security, education, health research, foreign aid, environment, transportation…those surging costs of the big 3 create a moral hazard. The more they increase, the less there is for our remaining budget. It's like a stack of garbage getting too big, too fast.

The only choice for Congress is to enact budget programs and step up to the plate by cutting spending. Congress should enact 20-year budgeted programs and review them every 5 years. There should be cut offs that do not allow the spending trends to exceed certain amounts. It is simple but effective. I don't see anyone else coming up with any sort of plan that makes sense and actually reduces spending apart from Paul Ryan. Republicans need to fight the liberal media and show the American people that conservatives are the party of solutions. Otherwise at some point down the road, kiss the entitlements goodbye.

Tax the rich or tax cuts? Who's right?

Taxing the rich as much as possible has its roots in…you guessed it socialism. The Marxist, socialistic economic principles really come to life on 2 main points:

1. The world's wealth is a fixed quantity: Absolutely not true. There is NOT a finite amount of money out there in the world. Just because someone is earning a million dollars does NOT mean that another person can't earn a million dollars. Money is NOT transferred from one person to another. In summary it's NOT a zero sum game. What liberals don't seem to understand is that when people make money and have success, their success benefits the lives of everyone around them. When people have money they add to the economy through investments and production. Another benefit of having money is consumption. When you accumulate wealth you accumulate goods, which is to the benefit of the person selling those goods.

2. The rich live upon the poor: This is fundamental to the liberal agenda that stops at nothing to make the American people believe it is true. "They say there are two Americas, one that does the work and another that reaps the reward. One America that pays the taxes, another that gets the tax breaks. One America that is struggling to get by and another America that can buy anything it wants." These words were from the ruthless trial lawyer John Edwards. Liberals have been promoting the agenda of class warfare for a long time. The landing point of this lie falls squarely on the rich. This lie is repeated and backed up by the media, the government and the confused people of the United States. It is the foundation of the Democratic Party. Tax the rich as much as possible and everything will be ok. Tax the corporations and blame them for our problems.

Liberals continue to propagandize how the gap between rich and poor is putting an end to the middle class. I beg to differ. According to the Book, *The End of Prosperity,* "the purchasing power of the median income family, that is, families at the midpoint of their income continuum, rose to $54,061 in 2004 an $8,228 real increase since 1980. The middle class is not disappearing…it is getting richer." Fortunately for us, it's not just the middle class that's getting richer but also the entire nation, including the poor. We have all made great strides in creating a better life. "The End of Prosperity" points out again, "more wealth was created in the United States over the past 25 years than in the previous 200 years." We've seen an increase in real dollars from 25 trillion in 1980 to 57 trillion in 2007. That's a staggering amount of increase and it should make all of us proud. A recent study from the Congressional Budget Office in May 2007, showed that from 1994-2004, the poor had the highest increase in income. The poor are improving faster than any other segment of America. Unfortunately, we don't get the news reported to us in a fair and balance way (except Fox news). It is hard to say that those 40 million Americans who are living below the poverty line are really poor compared to those living in third world countries. Poor people of the United States: 75% have a car, 78% have a DVD players and 62% have cable or satellite TV and 80% have air conditioning. If you asked someone from India or Africa if having a place to live, food to eat, a car, television and air conditioning meant you were poor -you would probably get a pretty disgusted look from them. A poll by Rasmussen showed that by a ratio of 6-1, (poor) families had enough to eat and lived in a house or apartment in good repair. Not only are the poor people of America getting by, they live substantially better lives than those of the middle class just 30 years ago. The average consumption of vitamins and minerals is virtually the same for the poor and middle class today. The poor also enjoy more comforts and are as healthy as the middle class. What makes things even more impressive is that the Census Bureau Figures also include illegal and legal immigrants, which account for ¼ of all the poor in America. Fortunately, for most Americans being poor is a transitive problem. The majority of people who are poor do not remain so. The most important factor in determining levels of poverty is age. Those just starting out in the workforce have a lower salary but over time they become more knowledgeable, acquire more skills and ultimately increase their income. When you work hard and take advantage of opportunities your income increases and your life improves.

The mantra of wealth distribution making society a better place comes only from the left. Since Obama is the most liberal senator ever elected to the presidency, it is no wonder he backs this idea. Liberals believe that if everyone took home the same amount of money the world would be a utopia. It is as if there would be no problems and social unrest would be a thing of the past. As we all know, life isn't perfect and nothing is ever equal. People need to understand and grasp this fundamental fact: when opportunity is taken away, freedom is taken away. When the state tells you how much you'll make, or when you'll have a vacation, you are not free. When the state says- no matter how much you work, your pay will only be the same- incentive is taken away. The inability to understand these points leads to frustration and confusion. If I worked at a government office that told me I'd never get ahead and I would never make more than $50,000 no matter how good I was at my job I would be incredibly frustrated! Life would be so boring. Plus, since I couldn't get ahead what is the point in working anyway. I would barley do enough to call it working. I would work the least amount I possible could while still collecting money. After all, it really doesn't matter because all my incentives were taken away. I would probably stop working entirely and just collect government checks for sitting on my ass. This is a sad, empty, terribly frustrating way to live and that's what other countries have been saying for as long as they have been countries. This is *one* reason why Greece is completely broke. When the government takes away your opportunity and tells you how to live and commands you like a robot, a part of you is taken away. I really hope people see government as a scary thing that impedes your success in life. Government cannot create a better life for you; it only succeeds in keeping you dependent upon it. If liberals were able to see government in this light perhaps they wouldn't be so quick to endorse it. When people can see government for the control freak that it is, then and only then, will people wake up and realize their freedom has been stripped away.

Tax cuts help every segment of America

We can't keep the current platform of endless debt, run away spending and over the top entitlements. The Bush tax cuts are a great example of a way to increase government revenues which we obviously need since our government is broke. In 2003 when he began slashing rates, revenues increased 18% of GDP by the year 2007. This brought in higher levels of federal revenue, NOT lower, as every liberal would have you think. Not until 2009 did revenues fall and that had to do with the horrible 2008 economic crash bringing everyone's income down with it. Government gets more money when taxes are cut. Tax cuts from Kennedy, Reagan and Bush eras all provided more money going to the government every single year from 1961-2009. Even when Reagan reduced the top marginal tax rates from 70% to 28%, the amount of dollars collected in taxes went up significantly by the time he left office. America is built on the foundation that if you work hard and obey the laws you will be able to keep the majority of your hard-earned money. In the recent months we've been confronted with the old but repeated mantra every American needs to pay their fair share. This only comes from the liberal side of America. Why do liberals continue to demand that Americans pay more in taxes when we already do? This mantra is repeated ad nauseam, that the rich get away without paying taxes and the poor are left to bear the brunt of them; that if everyone chipped in more and gave more of their hard earned money to the government then America wouldn't be broke. Liberals say Americans need to pay their fair share. Now if you say this, that's means by definition that you want to make things equal. If you want to make things equal then you view things from a socialistic approach to produce economic equality. How can it be "more American" to cough up more of your own money? It is, however, more socialistic to give up your money. Why can't liberals just say it?

Before we go accusing the rich of not paying their fair share let's make sure we know who pays their fair share and who doesn't. The top 1% pays 35% of taxes and the top 10% pays 70% of all federal income taxes! Let's see here—the top 10% pays 70%...hardly seems fair for the 10% does it? So I'm not sure where the, liberal mantra of "tax them more" comes from. That hasn't stopped Democrats in office from trying to spin this debate and play class warfare games while trying to influence the American people. Here is a quick example: Say you were coaching a high school football team that had 50 players on your squad. Take the top 10% of your most productive players and tell them they should be responsible for doing 70% of the work. Those 5 guys (10%) would not be very thrilled because they wouldn't have enough help from the other 90%. If those 5 guys were told, "Hey why are you so selfish and only doing 70% of the work? Those 5 players would be in shock and probably say you are ridiculous. Well that is exactly what is happening. Many Americans don't have time to straighten out all the lies that come out of the White House. When you have liberals screaming from the rooftops time and time again, it reaches a certain percentage of people who then believe the lie is true. The other piece of the puzzle is the other 20% who don't pay anything in taxes and in fact pay negative 6.6%; this according to the CBO in 2009 (which data was collect through 2006). The bottoms 20% actually receive more money back through tax credits than they put in! It gets worse. The bottom 40% contribute negative 3.6% in taxes making the top 60% pay the equivalent of 103.6% of all the taxes collected. Talk about a group not paying their fair share. Even if the Federal Government took every single penny from the top 1% (which we know would never pass through Congress) that would yield our government less than 2 trillion dollars. That happens to be what the Obama administration spends in 1.6 years. Heavy taxation of the ultrarich won't get us out of our current debilitating amount of debt. Instead, it comes back to government spending less and reforming entitlement handouts. Our current administration is bent on destroying the rich through heavy taxation instead of providing incentives to help others and create a better life for themselves. Heavy taxation only serves to deter productive citizens by penalizing hard working people. This theory is a product of social engineering because it tips the balance of power to the government by forcing the hard working citizens of America to redistribute more of their hard earned money to those who don't work. If liberals could stop seeing business as the enemy, maybe it would help clarify people's feeling on our current situation. Take for instance the "99%" who are marching, chanting, complaining, defecating on cars and in general completely confused on why they are so angry. These people are calling for reform of Wall Street and big business. They are angry with corporations, yet everything they own and spend money on is made from a big corporation. Remember every big corporation was once a small business. The reason businesses "made it big" was because they worked hard had a little luck and made strategic financial decisions which enabled them to succeed. Besides, in some form or another their product was in demand and improved the lives of those who bought that product or service.

Liberals believe that if you raise tax rates by say 15% then the federal government will collect 15% more in revenue than before. In the real world life doesn't work this way because humans are creative and find ways to improve their lives, despite government always trying to make it harder. Incentives shift when tax rates change. Instead of wealthy people continuing to invest, a tax increase causes their incentive to change and place their money elsewhere (say tax- free municipal bonds) to avoid the heavy 15% increase. Even though our government thinks we are stupid, many of us can think for ourselves. In fact we are probably smarter, especially when it comes to keeping our hard-earned money. We might not know all the little details of every piece of legislation nor do we have time to keep up with the endless red tape of regulation (which only causes you to lose more time and money) but we do find legal ways to reduce our tax burden, to which there is evidence of this throughout history. To keep things simpler lets look at the time period from 1950-2009. This era saw federal tax receipts average 18% of GDP and max out at 20.6% of GDP. The average was 18% despite federal taxes on the top margin ranging all across the board from as high as 92% to 28%. The amount the federal government collected basically didn't change. Why, because the incentives changed. This leads us to an obvious conclusion. Tax reform! Reform has been needed for long time and now is as good of a time as ever to make this a reality. Please somebody, anybody, make the flat tax happen! Take 15% and apply it to every single living human being in America. No loopholes, no special interest groups getting deductions, no secret back room deals, no fancy accountants to get anyone out of the 15%. It's so simple, so easy and it will save the American taxpayer valuable time. Our current tax code has a ridiculous amount of words, 9 million to be exact. Burn the tax codebook and replace it with…Pay your 15%. This is way too simple and easy right? Hopefully it will happen someday and make our lives much easier.

How about the Flat Tax

Our current system is too complicated and filled with special tax loopholes. The flat tax could eliminate loopholes and at the same time get rid of all the influence special interest groups have in maneuvering around the system to escape paying taxes. The flat tax makes things fairer and puts America in a much more competitive situation in the global market. Our current tax system has 893 forms but the flat tax would require only 2! And unlike our current system, which punishes people for contributing to the nation's wealth, a flat tax would lower marginal tax rates and eliminate the tax bias against saving and investments, thus ensuring better economic performance in a competitive global economy.

A flat tax would include:

-One single rate of taxation

-No death tax

-No capital gains tax

-No double taxation of saving

-No double tax on dividends

-Territorial taxation

Households would receive a generous exemption based on family size. For instance, a family of four would not begin to pay taxes until its annual income reached more than $30,000.The individual postcard is so simple that a third-grader could file a family's tax return in about five minutes. A flat tax would treat people equally. No longer would the tax code penalize success and discriminate against citizens on the basis of income. In the end, the amount of taxes collected by the federal government would not depend on the maneuverability of lawyers, lobbyists, and accountants on the payroll.

5 conservative points to put America on the right path

1.) Reduce spending

We need a spending cap of 20% of GDP: if we don't make targets then we automatically go into spending cuts across the board. We make it so no one can touch this target. We enact cuts across the board for everyone. Straight cuts are better than a deficit targets because, they allow for big tax hikes, which will further put us into stagflation. Liberals say well lets just tax the rich. Remember, if we taxed the rich a 100% it still wouldn't come close to the amount of money needed to get us out of this mess. Besides, the rich always find ways to greatly reduce the amount of taxes they owe with the help of powerful lawyers. The rich didn't become rich by accident. They are smart and they have smart people working for them. They will not just throw money away without a fight.

The Federal Reserve likes to use the term quantitative easing but we all know what this means: the excessive printing of money. Our Federal Reserve is doing this right now with complete disregard for the American people. The Fed believes, that if you don't have enough money to pay it back, just print more money. The problem is, you will inflate away tremendous amount of wealth. You destroy wealth with inflation and that's where the United States is heading. When talking about tremendous debt, just look at Greece for instance. However, Greece's problem is actually a little better for them in the long run because they can't just print more euros. In a way this is good for them, because they are forced to cut spending or go into default. For the United States, quantitative easing is only prolonging the pain for some future date down the road.

2.) Reduce Regulation

Regulation is stifling growth and putting a chokehold on the economy. Here are examples of truly harmful and dangerous regulation that is starting because of democrats. Too much regulation leads to corruption because everyone wants a piece of the pie. Liberals are in favor of heavy regulation because they believe someone needs to "oversee" all that goes on in the market place and think that a lack of regulation will lead to chaos if someone isn't there to "regulate" things. They forget that too much regulation places a huge burden on small businesses and increases prices.

Want higher electricity prices? Guess what they are coming to a house near you. Thanks to the utility maximum achievable control technology (MACT) standards and the cross state air pollution rule (CSAPR). One thousand power plants will be affected and so will your electricity bill. In many areas around the country, people can expect their bills to go up anywhere from 12 to 24%. This is due to the EPA and democrats. As I will show you later in the book, the notion of greenhouse emission is the most over hyped, nonexistent problem ever created by central planners to expand their influence and fatten their pocket books at the America people's expense. Furthermore, power plants emit water vapor! Yet this hasn't stopped Obama's regulatory agenda. In the beginning of October 2011, the boiler MACT rule will begin causing an unnecessary burden for places that use boilers including hospitals, factories, businesses and universities. The Environmental Protection Agency's strict regulatory requirements will cost American's billions of dollars in compliance costs; increase the costs of goods and services, at the same time risk losing over 200,000 jobs. Thank you yet again, EPA. Insert sarcasm…now. Also starting October 3rd, 20111 the "cement MACT" will affect every single cement plant in America by forcing all plants to comply with more job crushing regulations. Not only will this increase costs but also it will make sure that thousands lose their jobs as companies are forced to use overseas labor. Think about it, cement is used in virtually every single infrastructure project in the United States. Alabama recently put a 350 million dollar production facility on hold due to the EPA's ridiculous restrictions and stopped 1,500 American citizens from obtaining a job.

The coal/ash restriction is set to begin October or November costing 100's of billions of dollars. This rule affects all areas of business development from concrete production to building projects across America. Greenhouse Gas rule from the EPA will stifle job production and increase cost in every form of energy we use. The EPA's new source performance standards (NSPS) will affect new and existing oil, natural gas, coal fired power plants and oil refineries nationwide. Again, a complete slap in the face to every single American since its merit is based on 100% fraudulent evidence of emissions that only serves to empower the EPA, liberal leaders and "greenwashing" party leaders in the UN and America.

3.) Simplify tax code

I think once America can get a firm grip on what the flat tax brings to the table I believe we can really move towards tax reform. A flat tax would bring money into the Federal Government with no loopholes. You pay what you pay. Tax reform is a large task and unfortunately, one that will not take place overnight. *A flat tax would include:* One single rate of taxation, no death, no capital gains tax, no double taxation of saving, no double tax on dividends and territorial taxation

4.) Continue tax cuts - The world's wealth is not a fixed quantity

Money is NOT transferred from one person to another. In summary, wealth is NOT a zero sum game. After the 2003 Bush tax cuts (03-07) tax revenues grew 500 billion. In 2003 when he began slashing rates revenues increased 18% of GDP by 2007. This brought in higher levels of Federal revenue, NOT lower, as every liberal would have you think. Not until 2009 did revenues fall and that had to do with the horrible 2008 economic crash bringing everyone's income down with it. Government gets more money when taxes are cut. Tax cuts from Kennedy, Reagan and Bush all resulted in more money going to the government in every single year from 1961-2009. By the time Reagan left office, the amount of dollars collected by the federal government increased significantly when he reduced the top marginal tax rate from 70% to 28%. America is built on the foundation that if you work hard and obey the laws you will be able to keep the majority of your hard-earned money. What no body seems to talk about is this: raising taxes hits *earnings not wealth.* This hurts the people who are trying to become rich. People don't get taxed for being rich; taxes attack people who are trying to become wealthy.

5.) Major entitlement reform

Clearly we need reform and it's going to come down to cutting benefits. Something no one wants to hear but must accept. America cannot continue on its current path. The average household spends 50 times more than they did on healthcare than in 1960. In the 60's we used to spend 5.6% of our economy on healthcare. That has now risen to 17.6%, a major difference. Currently we have 10,000 baby boomers being added to Medicare everyday! We can choose to do nothing and this socialized program will run out in 9-10 years. The price tag will almost double over the next 10 years, going from around 550 billion to 980 billion in Medicare. Medicare's problem huge problem is too much spending. But it also lacks any sort of competition and innovation. Competition and innovation are the only solutions that are capable of turning around this out of control bus. Our national debt is expected to be twice as large as our economy in 2030 with Medicare playing the largest role.

A key point in the premium support plan is to know that it would grow at the current rate of inflation. The important point is this- it would put pressure on insurance to keep costs down and help keep the programs growth rate in check. The numbers reveal much needed improvement. Ten years after implementation, the federal government would spend about 240 billion less per year on Medicare and after those first 10 years the cost of Medicare would actually decline as a share of GDP. By 2040 the CBO shows a savings of 900 billion per year! The only choice for Congress is to enact budget programs and step up to the plate by cutting spending. Congress should enact 20 year budgeted programs and review them every 5 years. There should be cut offs that do not allow the spending trends to exceed certain amounts. It would give us a fighting chance to keep entitlements without letting them steamroll us later down the road.

It should be quite clear to everyone by now that we desperately need a regulatory rollback and flat tax reform to boost asset prices, to get banks to loan, to get companies to invest and America back to work. It is also quite clear that these ideas are exactly what liberals and this current democratic administration keep preventing from coming to fruition.

E is also for "Energy"

Energy is the number one resource that nations will fight over in the coming century. As we have seen in the past years, the United Nations is sure interested in telling every country what energy they should and should not use. It is a shame because those on the left have gone along with this and are completely on board with transforming our nation's energy supply. On the other hand, Republicans want to use the energy we have since everything we need is right here in our own land. Let us take a look at the resources we have, how much we have and why we aren't using them.

What is going on with the United States energy supply?

The energy sector is a 5 trillion dollar global business. That is an incredible amount of money. The power struggle between which countries produce what will ultimately decide who becomes the next super power of the world. America has the largest reserves of coal, natural gas and oil when combining these 3 life-changing fossil fuels. According to the Institute for Energy Research, we have more than 1.4 trillion barrels of oil that is recoverable in the United States with existing technology. We surely have more oil than all of the Middle East combined. The Obama administration knows we have over a trillion barrels of recoverable oil and yet they continue to distort the facts by telling the American people,

"The United States only has 2% of the world's oil yet uses 25%." The Obama administration claims this 2% garbage by only counting the areas his government has allowed companies to drill. We have the most oil in the world and its time to start using it! What has kept us from obtaining new oil leases to begin drilling in our most abundant sites? The EPA and liberals! The EPA is a ruthless organization that stops at nothing to prevent businesses from obtaining new drilling leases. Whether it's the endangered lizard, frog or bird, the EPA finds a way to restrict our drilling and make sure we don't start new projects. Even when research has shown that no animal is being hurt, they continue to prevent new permits for extraction of fossil fuels. To carry the point even further, animals such as the Alaskan moose have actually increased since the Alaskan pipeline was started because of the heat it generates, providing a great family home for those animals. The truth is of no importance to environmentalists and it hurts the American people every time liberals prevent America from drilling.

America's Natural Gas, Coal, and Oil

We are number two in the world in natural gas reserves. The great thing about natural gas is that it provides high power density at a low cost. It enables the United States to provide enormous quantities of energy to large amounts of people. We have more natural gas than the Saudis have oil. Natural gas is vital to our nation and has the added benefit of automobile use as well. The United States is the world's leading producer of coal, which generates vast amounts of energy. We also have a decent amount of power plants in the United States. They are clean, safe and an effective source of energy but liberals have shut down our ability to obtain new permits. Conversely, wind and solar account for only 1% of all our energy needs and are inefficient as well as costly.

Natural gas is so abundant in the United States that estimates show that the United States has enough to last us over 100 years. That is at the low end. Other estimates illustrate our reserves at around 30,000 trillion cubic feet or enough to last around 280 years. Around the year 2000, so-called energy experts forecasted that the United States would be in trouble by the 2020. Meaning we would have to double our imports to meet the demand by that time. They were way off. The department of Energy shows that natural gas reserves will grow by another 20% over the next 10 years. Hydraulic fracturing is the reason and is showing huge promise for recovering natural gas and oil. In August 2011, exciting news came out of the Marcellus Shale Formation in West Virginia. New estimates are calling for 500 trillion cubic feet of natural gas. Geologists insist that horizontal drilling and hydraulic fracturing methods, which were previously used in the Barnet Shale of Texas, will generate at least 50 trillion cubic feet of recoverable natural gas or more. That well alone has the ability to provide all of the United States for 2 plus years and has a value of about 1 trillion dollars! It is estimated that Ohio, which has been hurt by so many people leaving for bigger cities like Chicago and New York and Washington D.C. will have an estimated 200 billion dollars pumped into the state for its share of the shale profits.

For those far left liberals nervous about the technique of fracturing, do not be. In fact, if you had been paying attention, this technique is nothing new. The practice has been around for close to 70 years, dating back to the 1940s. Seventy years is a long time and of course the procedure has been refined (no pun intended) over those years and used well over 1 million times. This procedure alone has helped bring up billions of barrels of oil and hundreds of trillions of cubic feet in natural gas. Steve Hayward of the Weekly Standard has documented that shale gas accounts for 20% of United States gas production and that 80% of new natural gas wells drilled in the next decade will take advantage of hydraulic fracturing.

According to Americansolutions.com, "lawmakers reps Diane DeGette (Democrat Colorado) and Jared Polis (Democrat, Colorado) have introduced legislation (the FRAC ACT) that would put the United States Environmental Protection Agency in charge of regulating hydraulic fracturing despite the fact that fracturing has been effectively regulated at the state level for decades." Additionally, senators Bob Casey (democrat, PA) and Chuck Schumer (democrat, New York) have introduced anti-drilling legislation in the Senate. This is a blatant attempt at shutting down fracturing drilling and the EPA has the power to do just that. Originally, studies on fracturing were done to make sure our drinking water was not impacted (which was a good thing) but by turning it over to a federal agency, filled with anti drilling procedures, you can bet the house that the EPA will do everything in its power to slow or even shut down shale gas production. State regulators have already provided the necessary oversight and have made sure the drilling is safe. Even former President Bill Clinton admitted that fracturing is safe and supports efforts to find natural gas this way sighting hydraulic fracturing has worked in his home state of Arkansas. Independent studies have shown two very important findings. One, the EPA has already investigated hydraulic fracturing under President Bush and found nothing wrong. There was no indication what –so –ever that drinking water became contaminated. Point number two is the Groundwater Protection Council (GWPC) released a study in 2009 showing that it is basically impossible for fracturing to contaminate drinking water. To further show the hidden agenda behind the EPA, the Interstate Oil and Gas Compact Commission (IOGCC), an association of state regulatory agencies stated the drinking water to be safe. Of course this hasn't slowed the EPA from their wild goose chase of making fracturing illegal. They are still preparing legislation to remove fracturing and make this wonderful, clean, safe technique outlawed.

Despite all the benefits fracturing provides for the America people, the EPA persists on looking for anything they can find to derail oil and gas projects. In the case of fracturing the EPA has falsely turned to accusing the release of chemicals during the process of retrieval. Once again the evidence has shown otherwise. The website fracfocus.com shows that chemical extraction is not a problem. They point out that chemicals serve many functions in hydraulic fracturing; from limiting the growth of bacteria to preventing corrosion of the well casing, chemicals are needed to insure that the fracturing job is effective and efficient. The number of chemical additives used in a typical fracture treatment depends on the conditions of the specific well being fractured. A typical fracture treatment will use very low concentrations of between three and twelve additive chemicals, depending on the characteristics of the water and the shale formation being fractured. Each component serves a specific, engineered purpose. For example, the predominant fluids currently being used for fracture treatments in the gas shale plays are water based fracturing fluids mixed with friction reducing additives (called slickwater). The addition of friction reducers allows fracturing fluids and sand, or other solid materials called proppants, which are pumped to the target zone at a higher rate than if water alone were used. As well as friction reducers, other additives include: biocides to prevent microorganism growth and to reduce biofouling of the fractures; oxygen scavengers and other stabilizers to prevent corrosion of metal pipes; and acids that are used to remove drilling mud damage within the wellbore area. These fluids are used to create the fractures in the formation and carry a propping agent (typically silica sand), which is deposited in the induced fractures to keep them from closing up. In classifying fracturing fluids and their additives it is important to realize the service companies that provide these additives have developed a number of compounds with similar functional properties to be used for the same purpose in different well environments. The difference between additive formulations may be as small as a change in concentration of a specific compound. Although the hydraulic fracturing industry may have a number of compounds that can be used in a hydraulic fracturing fluid, any single fracturing job would only use a few of the available additives.

What about coal?

As of 2006, coal provided 41% of the world's total electricity. 41% is by far the biggest share of electricity production in the global market. Natural gas comes in at a distant second place at 20%. Coal is an extremely value resource that America just happens to have in abundance. I recently read about the Cardinal Mine in Kentucky. It is the 35th largest mine in America and produces 6 tons of coal per worker per hour. It produces the raw energy equivalent of 66,000 barrels of oil per day, a significant amount of energy. The one mine in Kentucky, ranked 35th, equals the daily output of all solar panels and wind turbines combined in the US! In 2008, the US produced 52,026,000-megawatt hours of electricity from wind and 843,000-megawatt hours from solar for a total of 52,869,000-megawatt hours. This equals 88,300 barrels of oil per day. What does that mean? That means one single coalmine produces 75% as much raw energy as all the wind turbines and solar panels in the United States. That truly is remarkable and points to two important things; first it's hard to realize just how much energy we use in a given day. Second, coal is vastly superior at producing energy than solar and wind combined. Yes, it is true that coal release too much mercury, lead and other heavy metals into the air and streams. Yes, coal plants need to be cleaned up. But they are responsible for enormous outputs of energy and are the leading supplier of electricity around the globe. If you reduce coal, you replace it with what? Tell China and India to reduce their output since they are two of the three leading users of coal for electricity. The answer is not to just shut down every coal plant across America, but that is exactly what liberals want to do - completely remove coal from the energy equation.

Unfortunately, America cannot count on the left-leaning government officials to actually help us. Ken Salazar, who heads the Department of Interior, overseas all domestic oil and natural gas production on federal lands (which is most of America, since the federal government owns almost all of it). He is a part of the most anti-drilling administration in the history of United States government. Salazars' record demonstrates again and again how he has denied or delayed leasing opportunities for drilling. To add insult to injury the administration also imposes taxes on oil and gas companies for lack of production despite the fact that it's the Department of Interior that's responsible for the delays! This stance by liberals is not only anti-drilling, but anti-energy independence and once again, anti-job. It is not hard to imagine how easily this department works along side the EPA. One would think its sole purpose is to stop drilling all together. This just might be the case. Democrats are stifling our production of homegrown energy for really no reason at all. This stance goes beyond frustrating and becomes plain scary. We know liberals want expensive oil and high gas prices. We know this because they've told us. They've told us that riding our bikes is the wave of the future. Liberals have told us that high-speed rail is the answer, despite no one every riding it and the federal government subsidizing almost all it. However, we know this is wrong. Oil, gas and coal are plentiful here at home. On top of which these natural resources don't hurt our planet. In fact they've done wonders to enrich our lives in so many ways. If we can strip back the layers of legislation that Democrats have proposed and help them realize that climate change is normal we have a chance at removing our dependence on foreign oil and gas. If we can show them that oil is just the remains of dead plants that have formed under pressure from 1000s of years ago and that the CO_2 they produce has absolutely no impact on the environment, maybe, just maybe we can forget about all this nonsense and get back to production. America needs to return men and women to work. Let us get back to common sense and rely on America for its energy instead of foreigners and radical countries like Venezuela and Saudi Arabia. Perhaps one day all of America will wake up. I know one thing for sure; we have a much better chance of this happening with Republicans in office.

Where does the U.S. get their most important natural resource, oil?

Reports on the news do not tell us where are oil comes from so the American people are left to wonder how much we are going to pay each year without knowing why. Let us set the record straight on where the U.S. gets its oil. According the United States Department of Energy the majority of our oil does not come from the Middle East. Although, one can easily see we have 3 dangerous enemies on that top 10 list. Liberals always comment that the United States is only involved in the Middle East for the oil…sorry, but that is just not the case. Here are the top ten countries that the U.S. imports from:

1.Canada
2. Mexico
3. Saudi Arabia

4. Venezuela

5. Nigeria

6. Angola

7. Iraq

8. Algeria

9. United Kingdom

10. Brazil

I don't know about you, but I only see three Middle Eastern countries in there (if you consider Algeria to be in the Middle East). According to DOE, the United States is the world's third largest crude oil producer, less than 40 percent of the crude oil used by United States refineries was produced in the United States. Net petroleum imports (imports minus exports) account for 58 percent of our total petroleum consumption. About 50 percent of our petroleum imports are from countries in the Western Hemisphere, with 19 percent from the Persian Gulf, and 18 percent from Africa and 13 percent from other regions." Oil is the number one commodity on planet Earth and it will be for the foreseeable future. Oil companies can barely keep up with the demand for oil from China and India- because their budding economies demand it. There will always be a buyer. No more excuses for not tapping into our abundant supply. Oil has improved the lives of every single American to an enormous degree. Oil is **not** bad for the environment and we need to drill in Alaska, Wyoming, the Dakota's and the Gulf of Mexico. This isn't even close to a serious debate. We have 250 million passenger cars and trucks and not tapping into our ridiculously rich reserves is an injustice to the American people.

The liberal energy agenda

Prices at the pump continue to be high. Energy prices are stifling economic growth and putting financial pressure on every American family. Energy is a necessity now more than ever. With so many people entranced by staring at their computers for hours on end, using air conditioning, relying on heat in the winter and gas for their car…our energy needs are more demanding than ever. The easy answer to this is drill for oil, drill for natural gas and continue to push for clean coal. Natural resources are America's bread and butter. Tennis might have its "big 3" in Federer, Djokovic and Nadal but America has a "big 3" of its own in oil, gas and coal. America has the largest supply of these three natural resources on the planet and through improved technology we will be able to find easier ways to extract them from the Earth. Whether the technique is through fracturing in North and South Dakota or improved oil sand extraction, the sky is the limit for our big three. Therefore, who keeps telling us we need to switch to wind and solar energy and why?

The Green Movement

The green movement, led by socialists and self-proclaimed communists, are at the head of the far-left green movement. If the goal of the green jobs czar is to find ways to produce less energy and much, much higher costs then, congratulations, you are doing it! As Secretary of Energy Seven Chu (who is responsible for the formulation of American energy policy) so aptly put it, "We have to figure out how to boost the price of gasoline to the levels in Europe." This liberal administration readily admits to wanting higher gas prices. Their thinking is that if gas prices go up, use will go down and it will be better for environment. However, you will see in the next section in great detail as to why this way of thinking cannot be justified. Just one scientific fact alone blows that whole argument out of the water: CO_2 follows warming; it does not create warming. It is impossible for CO_2 to be the driver of the problem. It's a main source of life, not a pollutant. Another comment by Chu shows exactly where the liberal agenda is headed. "Coal is my worst nightmare…we have lots of fossil fuels. That's really both good and bad news. We won't run out of energy but there's enough carbon in the ground to really cook us." This is an absurd comment and it falls right in line with what the liberals are supposed to say. Their agenda is not hard to figure out. Obama himself said, "Under my plan of a cap-and –trade system, electricity rates would necessarily skyrocket." That statement is very telling. It shows the plan front and center for Democrats. When it comes to energy provided by oil, coal or natural gas – Obama wants the price to go up. This is an anti-American stance to increase prices and reduce production, which means putting more people out of work. Liberals are so afraid of coal, which again, is tied to the imaginary problem of climate change. As the secretary of energy stated, "so if somebody wants to build a coal plant, they can –it's just that it will bankrupt them, because they are going to be charged a huge sum for all that greenhouse gas that's being emitted." As you can see, it all goes back to the Environmental Protection Agency's control over you. Democrats and the EPA are determined to tell the American people where their energy is going to come from. They are playing a political game with our future, our security and our pocket book. Another absurd comment came from the president himself, when he tried to pull one over the American people by saying we are pumping more oil than ever before. Thankfully, the American public knows by now that Obama is great at one thing – doubletalk. His comments were false, as we've learned that the increased oil production was only for a short time and only because his predecessors approved the type of drilling he has put a stop to! We all know this administration is full of "it", especially when it comes to the games they play with our energy. The liberal agenda has been to restrict oil exploration in the United States while additionally encouraging other countries to pull oil from the ground, give those countries billions to do so and then promise to buy that oil from them! Case in point when Obama promised this very same thing with Brazil in the spring of 2011. So, the United States should just smile and say yes, we will borrow more money that we do not have, to purchase "New stable sources of energy" from Brazil's offshore wells that we refuse to develop off our own shores. We aren't supposed to use are three biggest sources of energy because carbon could release into the atmosphere causing the world to set on fire and alter the temperature beyond the tipping point. It is irrational, unscientific and ties into the control grab by liberals as they push the nanny state dictate upon us.

One would think common sense would prevail but then again this is the Obama administration. The drilling ban and numerous restrictions placed on offshore and inland locations has put the American people out of work all because of fear of climate change. If this fear weren't front and center on the minds of the Environmental Protection Agency and the liberal elite, there wouldn't be any excuse to hold back drilling. According to Marketwatch, Attorney General Eric Holder created the Oil and Gas Price Fraud Working Group to, "Specifically monitor oil and gas markets for potential violations of criminal or civil laws." Sadly, this isn't a joke. Instead of drilling to provide jobs for millions of Americans, reducing our dependency on imports and reducing the price at the pump; the Obama administration is more concerned with finding people who have broken the law with oil and gas production. Even if the liberal cause is bent on destroying the production of American oil, gas and coal> the American public is not. 69% of Americans, according to a recent CNN poll (summer 2011) want more offshore drilling. That includes 56% of Democrats. If Obama wants to continue banning offshore drilling then he is being more than just anti-American. He is destroying jobs; increasing energy costs and increasing are dependency on foreign oil. It is a very destructive stance he has taken against the American people all in the name of the EPA and "global warming." The EPA has a major stake in environmental policies and is driven by the backing of climate change or fake global warming, as I like to call it. This one topic has dominated our energy conversation for the last forty years and its reached hysteric levels now. People are going to the Dr.'s office complaining of constant worry of "global warming." Every time you watch a program on the history channel, national geographic channel, discovery channel, PBS... (The list goes on) all you hear is whether or not our planet is overheating and if man has ruined the planet by pumping CO_2 into the environment. Through the grace of God, the world is finally finding out that "global warming" is fraudulent! It is the biggest scam put to the American public in the history of America's existence. Since this administration's vision of our energy future rests in the hands of academics and government bureaucrats bent on making up science as they go along we will continue to fight this battle until the America people fight back. As you'll see in the chapter on, "Discovering the truth on climate change," first find the truth and then help people see reality. Only then can we change our energy policy. Using oil, natural gas and coal allows us to use our own natural resources while reducing our dependency on enemy resources, without causing any harm to the environment. In fact the only by-product to coal, oil and natural gas is the continued betterment of everyone's life. Think for a moment what oil is. It is the dead remains of fish that over millions of years from the pressure of rocks and dirt, fashioned into a life-sustaining product called crude oil. Think how much our lives have improved because oil! What is coal? Coal is the product of millions of years of dead plants that through pressure have formed into another life improving product. Democrats always say they are for the poor and lower class. However, the left's "for the poor" statements are complete contradictions because if you were in favor of the poor you would be in favor of coal. Coal provides cheap, powerful energy at low cost -a cost that poor people can afford. In reality liberals always have been obsessed with population control and their commitment to reducing the world's population by protecting the planet has never been clearer. Part of the hysteria from the left comes from the idea of too many people, causing harm to the planet. As previously mentioned, one of the leaders of the "too many" movement was Paul Erhlich, who naturally was a professor at the Stanford University. The "too many" movements main point was that there are too many people taking up too many valuable scarce resources causing damage to the planet. Control is a major theme in the liberal agenda. As you can see, energy manipulation fits in perfectly.

What does clean, renewable energy bring to the table?

Global power consumption today is around 12 trillion watt-hours per year. Of that 12 trillion, 85% comes from fossil fuels. Moreover, by 2052 the world will be demanding an additional 10-30 trillion watt-hours per year. I firmly believe that wind and solar technology are not the answers to our energy needs. At least not for the next 100 years or so. Here are some reasons:

Wind power: incredibly inefficient and unreliable. The biggest problem with wind energy is that you can't store it! Wind energy comes and goes as often as the breeze in the air. As Science Magazine reported in 2009, "as the winds died down on a stretch of Texas that is filled with wind turbines and so did the energy output." Over a span of 3 hours the energy output was reduced by 75%, which is equivalent to a 1500-megawatt drop or the output of 3 midsize coal power plants. Wind power is subsidized by coal burning power plants since its tough to predict when and where the wind will die down. When that happens you can't just have the energy shut off, especially when it comes to commercial producers. If that happens, businesses cease to exist. Coal plants have become the safety net for wind turbines and they couldn't exist without coal. By placing climate change ahead of factual based science, they are in effect telling the American consumers, you can have your energy, but at a higher price and in a much more unreliable fashion.

Here are some keys facts about wind power:

a. As you have just read wind power is extremely inefficient. But did you know that it takes 2,000 new 750 kilowatt wind turbines operating at normal 28 % capacity to produce as much electricity as one 500 megawatt gas fired combined cycle base –load generating plant? This according to Doctors Fred Singer and Dennis Avery.

b. Predictions from the EIA projects predict that wind energy will supply only 0.0025% of U.S. electricity in 2020!

c. The development of wind farms helps those who build them not the American public. The price increase will show up in our monthly electric bills because of big government, big business and the greenwashing marketing.

d. The lie being told- that if we don't change from fossil fuel based technology then our planet will be in dire straights. This is a total bogus, unfounded argument and the reason we are being fed this lie is because of power and money. This lie is that if we don't reduce greenhouse emissions and find clean sources of energy, we will push the earth past the point of no return.

e. Wind turbines work well for one thing. Pumping water, which can be stored. That's how windmills became famous in the first place when they were used on American farms.

f. There are 400,000 birds killed each year due to wind turbines. You would think the environmentalists would go crazy over that one. They turn a blind eye to that because it conflicts with their ideology. When facts are not in their favor, they simply ignore them. When something as life changing as DDT comes along to wipe out Malaria and save millions and millions of children in Africa that would be a good thing, right! Not to left wing environmentalist. They say it wiped out populations of birds so they successfully got DDT removed from the market. Later it was found to have little or no impact on the bird population so why has DDT come back to the market and been used to save the children of Africa...Silence from the left is all you need to "hear."

Solar power fails to illuminate: 10 years ago there were around 500 solar panels in California. Now there are close to 50,000 according to the group, Environmental California. This will only run you $20,000 per rooftop. That's a tough sell to most Americans. It's hard enough to come up with a down payment, let alone an additional 20,000. This isn't the answer to the majority of the American people. Not counting rooftops, solar power represents a quarter of 1% of that state's total energy output. Furthermore the world's leader in solar power, Germany, only has 5,400 megawatts of solar power or 1% of their energy capacity.

One day we may very well be able to harness the sun's power for our energy needs. That day is neither today nor is it tomorrow. Yet this hasn't stopped liberal from trying. The United States government has given 3,156 grants for more than 6,300 projects to the tune of 1.33 billion as well as nearly 4.44 billion in solar investments in forty-six states. These grants come at a time when our government is broke and have all the energy we need in America with the big three. To substitute our bountiful resources for incredible inefficient solar technology is irresponsible, dangerous, and a crime against humanity, which ultimately hurts the poor much more so than those well off.

Around the year 2050 we will need an additional 10-30 trillion watts of energy. Using solar panels to produce this additional amount would require the United States to find 220,000 square kilometers worth of land plus the land for transmission lines, service roads, and maintenance yards among other needs. Windmills would require around 600,000 square kilometers. Much of the land required would reduce our forests to nothing and could not be used for farming. Basically, we would need the equivalent of all of South America and potentially need the land equivalent of China and India as well. That is totally outrageous. Talk about ruining the planet... all in the name of lies.

Power plants: In the future nuclear power will one day be a major player in the energy market. For now its relegated to the background, which is where, it needs to be. The good and the bad on nuclear power: The only thing coming out of power plants is water vapor. That is pretty good. They account for 20% of America's electricity needs and overall are a relatively safe way of producing energy. One ton of uranium produces more energy than is produced by several million tons of coal or several million barrels of oil. Another benefit to nuclear power is that it does not need large amounts of land to provide product power.

So why don't we have more of them? There are uranium shortages in the world for one thing. Also, we must be careful when storing nuclear waste at disposal cites such as Yucca Mountain in Nevada. Nuclear power plants need less fuel than ones that burn fossil fuels. There are a few downsides: nuclear power requires large amounts of water to be efficient. Nuclear plants are also expensive and need government help in the form of subsidies to function. Additionally, they take years to build and even longer to become operational. In 1975 the proportional uses of energy for electricity were spread out this way among the main 4: coal at 44.5%, natural gas at 15.6%, and oil at 15.15% and nuclear at 9%. In 2004 our electrical output was divided as such: coal 51.5%, nuclear at 20.8%, natural gas at 16.3% and oil at 3%. This is according to the U.S. energy Information Administration.

An advantage of nuclear energy for future purposes is what nuclear energy can provide hydrogen for fuel cells. Hydrogen by itself is not an energy source; however, it is an energy carrier. Operating at high temperatures, nuclear power plants could provide necessary energy to generate hydrogen. This hydrogen would then power fuel cells in electrical generators for cars, trucks, homes and commercial uses. Although France leads the world in proportional use, the United States has the most commercial reactors at 104. According to research, it has been estimated that the world contains enough uranium to last several hundred years. Between land extraction (which is easier) and sea extraction (which is harder but more abundant) uranium deposits are substantial but not overwhelming like oil. Thankfully, uranium deposits are spread out among different countries of the world and not just the Middle East. Canada and Australia rank among the leaders of the world in uranium deposits. Unfortunately, Jordan recently discovered a huge supply and China sits on a ton of uranium that they will be using to further their nuclear energy agenda. While fossil fuels remain plentiful and cheap world leaders will be content to keep uranium prices high as they seek to hoard them for future domestic energy or weaponry capabilities. It is perfectly clear where are energy focus needs to be – on fossil fuels. We can sustain our energy needs without importing from dangerous foreign countries and employ millions of workers here in America.

Liberals desperately want the American people to live a more simple life, especially the rich. The problem is, they have no idea just how much damage they are doing to the poor and the environment by trying to greenwash the American public. Imagine only having the use of a car 1-2 days a month. Electricity would be on a limited supply forcing restaurants and homes to curb the use of air conditioning. Think about the number of deaths that would come from poorly refrigerated food, or from the lack of high-tech diagnostic equipment barred from use. Enormous amounts of land would be destroyed along with the millions of trees and endangered species. Not only do liberals present the threat to our planet, but they also cause a threat to our overall existence. We would suffer unimaginable, painful deaths without the use of our natural resources, which liberals don't seem to grasp. Fossil fuels are a gift from God.

America wants: less government and fewer regulatory barriers in order to unleash the great American energy industry. If we do this, not only will we get the power to fuel the economy, but also will can create millions of new high-paying jobs. Support America's natural resources!

Who controls the energy for tomorrow?

There is a growing, scary agenda in American politics today, which will have a considerable impact on future generations. This agenda is happening in front of your face and you might not be aware of it. The agenda is to make you feel guilty and fearful of carbon emissions. This pressure to feel guilty plays itself out on the hearts and minds of individuals everywhere you look. Whether it is driving by billboard ads in California saying, "I will use less energy today" or the relentless commercials and TV stations touting how green they are, especially NBC, who practically shoves it down your throat. Our culture is going through a major shift and it's not because of sound scientific facts. Remember politics is a dirty game and energy is a huge issue. I hate to admit it but the Democratic, socialist agenda is slightly winning. One reason is because they have the backing of the media who is obsessed with finding alarmist stories. Another reason is the PR machine for the Democratic Party that is working in overdrive. There are two main ideas that are being pushed in the name of power and money. One, carbon emissions are bad and we must reduce them or risk losing the planet to a catastrophic meltdown. Two, we must switch to renewable, "clean" energy right now before it's too late. This is one of the main reasons I wrote this book. To push back one of the greatest lies that has ever been told. There is no global warming, but there is climate change. Climate changes all the time. It changed before humans were here and it will change after we are gone. The biggest claim by the liberal left is that we humans are causing the earth to warm because of our C02 emissions. This is not true for many, many reasons. Yet all it takes is one simple fact: **C02 follows warming, it does not create warming!** That one simple fact changes everything. Liberals either don't know this fact or won't admit it. To say that we are ruining the earth from all these carbon emissions is 100% false! Carbon cannot create warming, when it comes after it. It is like saying a home run happens before the pitch. Climate goes up and down and so does C02. If humans are warming the planet right now then how do you explain the alternating warm and cool periods during our past glacial periods? It was warming during the time of Jesus. Did they have millions of cars driving around the Gaza strip? No, of course not. C02 levels were 18 times higher during the Orvidician period, 490 million years ago. Was the industrial age in full swing then? I think not. There wasn't one single human being walking around then and C02 levels were 18 times higher and yet an ice age followed this time period. C02 in the atmosphere is only 0.001% of total C02 held in the oceans, surface rocks, air and soil. Yet these facts are ignored. The truth is brushed aside in favor of environmental agendas. The left does not want cheap energy. The left wants energy to be limited and expensive. When energy is cheap and plentiful it allows for life to flourish and individuals to thrive. It allows for people to produce more children and use resources. This is exactly what liberals are working so hard to prevent! That is a scary concept to environmentalists and not a good thing according to the left. In the course of the next 18 months the EPA will be unleashing a blistering attack on American businesses. More and more regulations on everything from coal powered plants to greenhouse gases, water intake, coal ash, smog and Mercury. The real point is to power *down* coal plants. Despite overlooking the fact that coal provides 45% of America's electrical power, the EPA will be forcing 1/5 of all coal plants to retire. Remember, this is for no good reason at all. According to the Edison Electric Group this will cost at least 129 billion.

Energy is such a high stakes, serious topic because dangerous countries have huge amounts of it. The United States is truly blessed with the amounts of natural resources we have. It is up to our leaders in Congress to put forth effective policies that will allow us to obtain and use our advantage of fossil fuels and keep us from depending on other nations that want to hurt, kill and eliminate us. Also, it is imperative for liberals to realize they are completely wrong about our abundant energy supply. They need to (for once) get on the right side of America and push for the use of oil, natural gas and coal. The big three help Americans find jobs, keep costs low and puts an enormous barrier between enemy countries while keeping us safe. Right now we are living in the greatest time in the history of the earth. We are in year 11,000 of the interglacial period and very lucky to have it this warm.

D stands for "Discovering" the truth on Climate Change

For the record, I used to believe in global warming. I was convinced that the earth was warming and got sucked in by media sensationalism. I didn't make time to research the topic until I sat down and had a chat with my father. I kept telling him, "listen to me, I've heard the reports and it really looks like our planet is in trouble." He told me, "I am not going to tell you what to think or what the right answer is but I do think you should spend some time and come to your own conclusion." I looked at the issue from both sides of the equation but nothing was adding up. After pouring over the research for years, I was never the same. I found lie after lie, leaving me with an incredible amount of frustration. So much frustration that I wasn't even able to sleep at night as my heart would continue to pound away at the eye opening information I kept finding. I felt as if I was a spy in East Germany walking around with some very important secret without a pulpit to shout from. The truth had been squashed in the name of manipulation and corruption and I had to share my revelation with anyone that was willing to listen. Anytime the subject would come up from then on out, I was determined to speak the truth and change minds. The liberal, democratic machine has been squashing America's freedom in the name of profit and control. If liberals get to tell every person what they should drive, where they can go, how much electricity they should use and that fossil fuels are bad, then government has you right where they want you. One could say they've been winning because they certainly have made people fearful. People are very freaked out about fossil fuels and the situation has only gotten worse. It has gotten so bad that people are actually going to psychologists, ridden with anxiety over a planet warming too much, too fast. Well, I am here to tell each and everyone human being on this planet, fear no more! Don't get me wrong, I love our planet and I'm 100% for the environment. I want clean oceans and healthy rain forests. I mean really, who wants pollution? Who is really in favor of over fishing? In fact I believe those that disgrace our planet should be reported, fined heavily and perhaps jailed. I probably care more about the disgusting practice of dolphin killing at places like the cove, more than anyone. We must protect this planet but not at the expense of corruption, manipulations and lies. Because man's C02 is not hurting planet earth and really has no impact at all. This uneducated bias toward C02 is at the core of every liberal, big government environmentalist. This anti C02 continues to be a great threat, not to mother earth, but to those trying to remain free and alive on this marvelous blue dot. My investigation into the world of climate change will hopefully change minds through factual history and accurate unbiased, professional research instead of science that has been skewed in the name of politics, money and power. Studying ice core samples 250,000 years ago off the ice shelves of the artic is like looking through a wormhole into natures past. When we take these samples off of Antarctica's Vostok glacier and measure the isotope levels it produces a clear historical picture of when warming and cooling has occurred throughout history and why. The collection of data from fossilized bee pollen, ancient tree rings, stalactites and stalagmites shows how ancient indicators help prove the small changes in the sun's irradiance. Through a mix of historical fact, unbiased scientific findings and evenhanded research I can prove to you that that indeed, warming and cooling is unstoppable.

Climate History and Dates

The earth is 4.5 billion years old. That's a long time to be around and the earth has seen a lot of change. 540 million years ago the earth went from an "ice ball" to a warm and humid world. 350 to 250 million years ago ice sheet reappeared at the higher latitudes while the earth only consisted of one large continental landmass – Gondwanaland located in the southern hemisphere. Over the course of millions of years Earth slowly separated through plate tectonics. Around the time of the dinosaurs, 60 million years ago earth went into a "greenhouse" condition because ocean circulation patterns were non-existent. At the time, Earth did not even have polar regions. As earth's plates continued to separate (as tectonic plates always do) Antarctica separated from South America giving way to the southern ocean around 30 million years ago. Skipping 25 million years to our current climate… 5 million years ago the continents give us our oceanic temperature conveyor belt in the North Atlantic. Moving forward to 2 million years ago we see the cycles in earth's relation to the sun producing alternating ice ages 90,000- 100,000 years and interglacial periods lasting 10,000-20,000 years. We are currently in one of these interglacial periods right now. Temperatures vary 5-7 degrees during these transitions and at times can change as much as 10-15 degrees.

Why would I bother going through earth's climate history. Because it shows us one thing- climate changes!!! Whether or not humans are here, climate will always change. Earth's changing climate is based on so many variables that it's hard to image, especially since they all must be taken into consideration all at the same time. Plus, variables constantly play off one another. The Earth changes are related to: the shape of the continents, shape of the sea floor, the pulling apart of the crust, stitching back together of the crust, opening and closing of sea ways, changes in Earth's orbit, changes in solar energy, supernova eruptions, comet dust, impacts by comets and asteroids, volcanic activity, bacteria, soil formation, sedimentation, ocean currents, chemistry of the air among others. It is ludicrous to think, humans putting some CO_2 in the air, would be way more important than all the incredible complex events happening at the same time. Additionally, CO_2 has a 600-800 year lag time. Meaning when warming occurs, it takes 600-800 for CO_2 to make an impact. That means everything we all arguing over right now doesn't mean a thing.

Let's jump all the way down to our modern day climate (our present day interglacial period) and focus on all the recent changes that have taken place on our earth. Authors Singer and Avery, in the book, *Unstoppable Global Warming every 1500 years*, break down the recent warming as follows: Climate forecasters must factor the 100,000 - year elliptical cycle, the 41,000 axial tilt cycle and the 23,000 "wobble" cycle, plus the 1500 -year solar- driven cycle. However, it is the 1500- year cycle that drives most of the Earth's climate change during interglacial periods like this one.

Recent Earth Climate History

1. 600 to 200 B.C.: Unnamed cold period that preceded the Roman Warming
2. 200 B.C. to about A.D. 600: Roman Warming
3. 600 to 900: Dark Ages cold period
4. 900 to 1300: Medieval Warming or Little Climate Optimum

1300 to 1850: Little Ice Age (two stages) the "little ice age" showed more floods, droughts, famines and storminess than warm periods. Yet we are told time and time again that CO2 is deadly dangerous and soon we will past the point of no return. Climate change means so much, because climate change means energy. What has happened since 1850 to present? Earth has warmed a little since 1850, about 0.8 degrees Celsius. The main surges of warming came from1850-1870 and again from 1920-1940. After 1940 temps declined until 1975, despite huge surges in industrial CO2 during that period. We should be extremely grateful that's its warmed up a little since the Little Ice Age part II because life is so much better for every single person on this planet when the earth is warmer. Humans thrive during warm wet periods and suffer immensely during periods of cold. Why is this big deal? This one topic alone has the power to change everything about your life. From the way you live, to what energy you use, to where you live, what job you take...

What is really going on, Climate Gate

We are being bombarded with two ideas: one that humans are killing the earth and two that the world is much worse off when it is warm as opposed to cold. The environmentalists have hijacked this topic in order to convince the entire planet that humans are to blame for the slight increase in temperature because of the release of so called "greenhouse gases" from fossil fuels, humans driving cars and methane from rice paddies among other things. Big government liberal brainwashing is seeping into every corner of the globe with their misguided notion that if we don't reform and stop the burning of fossil fuels we will destroy the earth and push the earth beyond its tipping point. They believe humans are destroying earth and that there are too many of us inhabiting this planet. Remember who is responsible for such a sick notion: big government liberalism and big business. Together they produce a frightening reality of endless regulation, stifling company growth, closing of American companies and the eventually relocation to China. If that weren't bad enough, big government's assault on economic growth combined with ridiculous amount of regulations not only means less economic freedom here but it also means the impending death of millions of third world civilians.

Where did it start? History of the Global Warming Myth

20,000 environmental activists convened with 2,400 official delegates at the Earth summit in Brazil in 1992. Their agenda – change the world's perception of fossil fuels from good to dirty. In order to accomplish this goal they needed a scapegoat and that scapegoat became C02. They framed the discussion around C02 as being a major pollutant in order to make the world believe C02 is heating the earth. In 1997 an international treaty took place in Kyoto, Japan, to convince every nation of two fallacies. One, that "greenhouse emissions" are destroying the earth and also to force every country into an agreement to reduce said "emissions" in order to save the planet. Stating this was "An insurance policy" for the earth. In order to make the Kyoto Treaty a reality, the world's scientists had to be on board with the idea that humans are damaging the earth and government action must be the solution. The IPCC set up their agenda- to make it appear as though man is responsible for global warming and it consisted of 4 main ingredients:

1. Manipulate their findings whether to fit their agenda
2. When their so-called evidence was found to be contradictory, they decided to push through with it anyway.
3. When findings didn't point toward man-made global warming they simply removed or added whatever data they needed.
4. When scientists expressed doubt they published their findings as though thousands of scientists agree even though IPCC papers were published with only 2 scientists signed on. They allowed for "back room" deals to go through and made their research point to where they wanted it to go.

The green movement hates cheap, abundant energy and will do or say most anything to get their message across. They believe in wind and solar technology despite it being ineffective and very expensive. Only common sense shows the correlation between allowing policies to stop the burning of fossil fuels and the death of billions of third world people. Half the world lives on less than two dollars a day. They don't have an extra $20,000 a year to put solar panels on top of their mud huts. Promotion of the greenhouse theory has allowed the EPA, green movement and liberals to call for restrictions and heavy regulation on any and all natural resources – fossil fuels. The greenhouse theory demands that energy be scarce and the agency that rations out that energy be very powerful. Therefore, the Kyoto Protocol was formed. It is an international agreement to limit the use of fossil fuel-based energy on earth. It never mentions if greenhouse gases would be dangerous to humans or the earth but nonetheless it was pushed through and negotiated by the Clinton administrations', Al Gore. The idea was put forth before his run for the President to give him something else to run on. Since the Kyoto Protocol didn't include developing countries, the United States Senate voted 95-0 in an overwhelming vote against harming

America's economy. It would have lead to job loss, major increases in energy cost and a significant trade disadvantage. Because European governments have heavily taxed their own energy for decades, they desperately want the United States to "go along with the program" so that we will be burdened with soaring energy costs just like them. Have you ever been over to Europe and gone to a gas station? It is shocking to see how much Europeans pay for gas. Well, it's a self-inflicted wound. They have significantly higher energy costs because they give themselves an unnecessarily high-energy tax – all in the name of fake global warming. The propaganda continues because highly qualified scientists run programs on computers, often leaving out "certain" factors. These same scientists get millions of dollars in research grants and must find ways to make their "evidence" come back looking the way their supplier wants it to look.

Sulfate Aerosol Fraud:

The IPCC – who is the supposed head of the global warming campaign decided that they needed to manipulate the "evidence" in their favor even when their "evidence" was contradictory. They formed ways to explain global warming as a man-made problem and used every trick in the book to make it look so. Acclaimed authors Avery and Singer point out the great inconvenience associated with the IPCC and the sulfate aerosol fraud in their book, *Global Warming Every 1500 Years*. Avery and Singer show through extensive research how the IPCC generated "findings" that backed up their position. For instance, the IPCC claimed that computerized models have show warming trends consistent with real world observations for the last 150 years. However, those real world observations didn't match up. Warming occurred in a slow erratic fashion with surges taking place from 1850-1870 and another surge from 1920-1940. Instead of a strong movement toward warming, like they thought would happen, a cooling trend took place in 1940. This did not sit well with the IPCC and they simply couldn't explain for the cooling. Since they couldn't explain the cooler factor in their greenhouse theory they just made up what could have accounted for the cooler. They blamed it on aerosol particles produced by emission from sulfur dioxide from electric power plants. They claimed that the aerosols counteracted the warming trend. The IPCC then published a second report in 1996, going on the record of accusing aerosols and stating that humans are indeed responsible for the warming. In 2001, a third report was published. Only this time the aerosols were in conflict with the findings. Because aerosols are at their uppermost when industrial activity is high then the northern hemisphere should warm more slowly then the southern hemisphere. The environmentalists claimed aerosols were responsible for reflecting sunlight- thus producing cooler temperatures in the northern hemisphere. However, observations showed the opposite to be true. Higher rates of warming occurred at the higher latitudes making their so-called findings in contradiction. Instead of admitting that computer models aren't even close at encompassing all the millions of variations that take place on Earth and in outer space, the environmentalists insisted that the aerosol idea was correct. In essence they basically said, who cares that the evidence doesn't show any correlation to man made warming, let's continue with this theory regardless of its accuracy.

After moving away from the aerosol idea the IPCC agenda continued to manipulate their research to make it fit their agenda. When encountered contradictory evidence they precede anyway. Its one thing to base your findings on scientific research, but it is quite another to just make it up. Not only has the IPCC taken out evidence when it doesn't show global warming but they put in fake evidence to boost their claim when they lack evidence. When it came time to publish their 1996 report from hundreds of peer reviewed scientific studies, their research came mainly from two research papers. One of the lead authors, Ben Santer, of the U.S. governments Lawrence Livermore National Laboratory had the same problem as the IPCC. He couldn't explain the upward trend occurring from 1940 to 1970. So instead of just reporting the truth, he simply deleted the evidence against global warming. Powerful people wanted to see the claims against fossil fuels validated, so they made sure no one had a problem with the deletion of evidence. He went ahead with the changes in the IPCC reports and is one of the main persons responsible for completely changing the world's perception of the issue.

Despite previous attempts by the IPCC and others to lie about global warming, they continued to manipulate and change facts. A 2000 Climate Change report from the IPCC erased a time period longer than the history of the United states, simply because it did not help the research of Michael Mann. He claimed that the medieval warming and the little ice age just didn't happen. Despite overwhelming evidence from tree rings, ice cores and mountains of research showing that these two time periods did in fact happen, the powerful, dishonest men, tried to delete it from the pages of history. How convenient! World temperatures dropped sharply from the year 1300 – 1850, around 2-4 degrees. This was a time filled with powerful storms, advancing glaciers forming, freezing cold temperatures and contrary winds, which plagued humans for over 500 years. Those opposing winds killed off Norse settlers of Greenland. It was a rough time to live on our Earth. And all in the name of power and money, liberals, the EPA and IPCC tried to report the research by deleting those two periods of time. They tried to say it never happened to slant their research in their favor. Not only does the IPCC manipulate evidence whenever they see fit, they exaggerate the amount of scientists who believe in this nonsense. Sometimes it's as few as two scientists stating their belief in global warming while tens of thousands come out against it. The IPCC states that all the scientists are on board when the majority of them really aren't convinced. In short, more scientists reject the idea of global warming than support it. Case in point: 17,000 scientists signed the "Oregon Petition" expressing doubt in man-made global warming. Ninety percent of United States climatologists state that global temperatures are due to a natural process. Ninety percent from another study of 400 climate researchers said there is absolutely no global warming going on. Half of those questioned do not trust forecast models.

Catching climate liars in the act

Just to take the point of "climate scientists" lying to the world, to an even higher level; here are some emails from the London Telegraph by James Delingpole, showing a series of profoundly incrementing emails written by so called "scientists", not in the name of science, but in the name of political exploitation.

Here are a few of those emails, courtesy of the Freedom of Information Act, 2011:

[/// The IPCC Process ///

<1939> Thorne/MetO:

Observations do not show rising temperatures throughout the tropical troposphere unless you accept one single study and approach and discount a wealth of others. This is just downright dangerous. We need to communicate the uncertainty and be honest. Phil, hopefully we can find time to discuss these further if necessary [...]

<3066> Thorne:

I also think the science is being manipulated to put a political spin on it which for all our sakes might not be too clever in the long run.

<1611> Carter:

It seems that a few people have a very strong say, and no matter how much talking goes on beforehand, the big decisions are made at the eleventh hour by a select core group.

<2884> Wigley:

Mike, The Figure you sent is very deceptive [...] there have been a number of dishonest presentations of model results by individual authors and by IPCC [...]

<4755> Overpeck:

The trick may be to decide on the main message and use that to guid[e] what's included and what is left out.

<3456> Overpeck:

I agree w/ Susan that we should try to put more in the bullet about "Subsequent evidence" [...] Need to convince readers that there really has been an increase in knowledge – more evidence. What is it?

<0714> Jones:

Getting people we know and trust [into IPCC] is vital – hence my comment about the tornadoes group.

<3205> Jones:

Useful ones [for IPCC] might be Baldwin, Benestad (written on the solar/cloud issue – on the right side, i.e anti-Svensmark), Bohm, Brown, Christy (will we have to involve him?)

<2495> Humphrey/DEFRA:

I can't overstate the HUGE amount of political interest in the project as a message that the Government can give on climate change to help them tell their story. They want the story to be a very strong one and don't want to be made to look foolish.

<3655> Singer/WWF:

We as an NGO working on climate policy need such a document pretty soon for the public and for informed decision makers in order to get a) a debate started and b) in order to get into the media the context between climate extremes/disasters/costs and finally the link between weather extremes and energy]

Please realize that this is political manipulation in the highest sense. The above emails are documented evidence of "leading scientists" who will do anything and say anything to further the false agenda of "global warming." It has to be stopped because the future of energy depends on it. The IPCC has finally gone on record admitting they have been wrong on "global warming." They reported that the reality of man-made warming claim was false. Of course this enormous "mistake" has never made its way to the media. Funny how that works...

Big government liberalism, big business and population reduction

Killing in the name of global warming; complete disregard for human life; zero respect for other cultures; murder for profit. They all mean the same thing when it comes the horrendous act committed by global warming enthusiasts, liberalism and big business. Thankfully American citizens still have some semblance of property rights. Unfortunately, for the rest of the world, the idea of freedom from big government mixed with corrupt agenda's for profit still runs rampant. Take for example, those poor Ugandans who were either burned to death, beaten or forcibly removed from their homes by government officers to clear land for New Forests Company to grow tree's in order to gobble up carbon credits. Because the (now laughable) idea of human induced climate change still presents opportunities for billion dollar business projects in the name of "protecting the planet," liberals see the murdering of innocent villagers as just some unfortunate event that must take place to save mother earth. This sick justification cannot continue. Please don't believe the media propaganda machine, which made a mockery of their report saying, "the settlers left peacefully and voluntary." The villagers tell a different story. Children were burned to death while their homes went up in flames. Others were beaten and illegally removed from their homes. We all can acknowledge that we must treat the earth with respect, limit pollution and strive for cleaner oceans. That is not what happened to those abused people of Kicucula Uganda. Big government liberalism invented the problem of global warming and big business ruthlessly snatched up the profit all at the expense of human life. New Forests, with investors like the World Bank and Hongkong and Shanghai Banking Corporation (HSBC) were granted a 50-year license to grow pine and eucalyptus forests in three districts after applying to the United Nations to trade under the format for carbon credits. Of course the United Nations was on board, since they consider themselves the leading authority of climate change under their branch called the United Nation International Panel on Climate Change. This wasn't the first time fake global warming has been used for extermination of humans and unfortunately it won't be the last. Isn't it time they get called out for it? Think about the needless murder of innocent civilians for a cause that does not even exist! Innocent victims continue to be killed and beaten in order to fatten the pockets of government officials, banks and corporations. Unfortunately for civilians across the globe, liberalism has always stood behind the idea of population reduction for the sake of the planet. If that doesn't make your blood boil, I don't know what will.

Just some facts, please! Courtesy of Doctors Avery and Singer: 20 profound facts from the highly acclaimed authors of *Unstoppable Global Warming, Every 1500 Years.*

Earth, sun relationship!

1. Earth's elliptical cycle around the sun changes every 100,000 years forcing the sun's radiation to travel 3% farther to reach our planet during the ice ages and reducing its intensity. Currently Earth's orbit is not very elliptical, and the variation between January's solar radiation and July's is only about 6%. When the orbit is more elliptical, the energy received can vary as much as 20-30%.

2. Earth's tilt changes every 41,000 years. At present, the axial tilt is about in the middle of its range.

3. Earth's wobble as it spins on its axis changes every 23,000 years. This precession is significant to the climate when the North Pole is pointed toward the star Vega, one of the brightest and nearest "landmarks" to Earth in the solar system. At that point the earth gets both harsh winters and hot summers. As the other extreme of the wobble when the precession puts summer at the "perihelion," the Earth gets milder summers and more winter ice sheets survive to the next winter. We now should be entering an extended period of ice sheet growth, according to the wobble cycle.

4. Climate forecasters must factor the 100,000 – year elliptical cycle, the 41,000 axial tilt cycle and the 23,000 "wobble" cycle, plus the 1500 –year solar- driven cycle. However, it's the 1500- year cycle that drives most of the Earth's climate change during interglacial periods like this one.

5. Antarctica has been cooling for past 30 years. The only part that is warming is the tip that points up towards equator. The rest of Antarctica has been getting thicker and stronger every year.

6. Medieval and Roman times had warming periods, much warmer than today without greenhouse gases.

7. Nitrogen – before man made industrial nitrogen, the world could only support 1.5 billion people. If the world went to organic farming we would have to clear half the worlds remaining forests.

8. Population growth has been a huge worry of activists. They need not worry. Births per woman in third world have dropped from about 6.2 in 1960 to about 2.8% and stability is 2.1. Thus poor nations have already come 75% of way to population stability. The "rich" nations are having 1.7 children per woman or less.

9. The United Nations predicts that world population will peak around 2040 or 2050 at somewhere between 8 and 9 billion. After that human numbers will slowly decline.

10. Glaciers: All around the world they show the same advance during little ice age and retreat during warm periods. It's a natural process.

11. We know that one ocean is actually getting colder. Scientists put weather balloons to the bottom and drag all the way up to the top. Although it was only the Atlantic Ocean that showed definite signs of getting colder. Also, sea ice in Antarctica is getting bigger.

12. Corn for ethanol is horrible. It drains aquifers but farmers get subsidy money so they don't care. Sugar ethanol (like in Brazil) is an option because it is better for the for the environment than corn ethanol. However, you need more cattle ranges, which in turn means cutting down more trees in the rain forest.

13. 1-3% of total CO_2 is from humans. Obama wants to enact the Kyoto agreement and that would reduce human output by 20-40% of 1-3%: meaning a total difference of 1.2%, which would have a max impact of 0.005 degrees Celsius change. This would cost us about 7 trillion and basically make us a third world country without changing anything because there is nothing that needs changing.

14. CO_2 from humans only stays in the air for four years.

15. Ordovician Period - time period that began 490 million yrs ago and lasted 50 to 80 million yrs. There was one continent, Gondwana, and a rich diversity of marine life. Though temperatures were much like those of today, CO_2 levels were up to 18 times higher than currently. In spite of the high CO_2 levels, an ice age occurred toward the end of period.

16. Ice melts slowly. Glaciers and ice caps can take 1000's of years to completely melt because their surfaces reflect away so much of the sun's heat. This is why the west Antarctic ice sheet, at least 10,000 years past its last ice age, still has another 7,000 years worth of ice to melt according to John Stone of the University of Washington. Even the melting of Greenland's ice sheet would only increase sea levels only 0.3 to 0.77mm per year. Meanwhile Antarctica would subtract 0.2 to 0.7 mm year because of increased precipitation added to ice caps.

17. 20,000 years ago sea levels were 400 ft lower than they are today. Sea levels have increased by 394 ft. since the last ice age began

melting some 21,000 yrs ago. By about 5000-6000 yrs ago most of the ice age's trillions of tons of extra ice had melted. After that, 3-4000 yrs ago global sea levels stabilized and no study has detected any significant acceleration during 20th century.

18. Holocene Climate Optimum - longest and warmest "warming" of the present interglacial, which occurred from 9,000 to 5,000 yrs ago. Greenland ice cores show temps then were 2.5 Celsius warmer then present 3,000 yrs ago. Laurentide ice sheet - huge ice sheet over much of Canada and northern U.S. during last ice age. Its five million square included parts of Iowa, Illinois, Indiana, and Ohio.

19. The length of sunspots cycles (range from 8-14 yrs) is even more accurate guide to the sun's warming than the number of sunspots, with longer cycles bringing more warming.

20. Because we are living in year 11,000 of the interglacial period we must remember to appreciate how lucky we are to be living in this time period. The last 11,000 years have see the greatest achievements of mankind in the shortest time period of all because of the remarkable warmth we humans have had during this period.

The world is immensely better off during periods of warmth as opposed to periods of cold and history backs this up. Take Greenland for example. When the Vikings settled upon Greenland it was called this for a reason. It was Green! Despite its far location to the north, Greenland was not covered in ice. Let me repeat that again. Greenland was not entirely covered in ice as it is today. The Vikings were pleased to find green grass, ice-free waters with codfish and seals in abundance. As Doctors Avery and Singer have so beautifully pointed out, the colony in Greenland grew to over 3,000 thousand people including 12 churches and they even had a bishop! Was this global warming? No, of course not! They were reaping the benefits of the medieval warming; a period that lasted from 900AD to 1300AD and made the northern part of Europe around 2 degrees warming than before. Generations of Vikings lived out their lives on Greenland longer than America has been a country. Think about the amount of wars that have been fought in this brief time period and it might allow for some perspective. As nice as the medieval warming was, the "little ice age" reared its ugly head from 1300AD to 1850AD and their time spent on Greenland was over. Ice began packing around Greenland and forced ships to take more southern routes to drop off supplies. Less hay could be harvested because of the cooler, shorter summers. The storms got worse and the ice got thicker. The last supply ship to reach the colony was in 1410 and then that was it. Battles insured with the Norse fighting off the Inuit hunters who came south to get away from encroaching ice in search in seals. When the cod went south in search of warmer waters things became unbearable. The skeletons in the graveyards showed smaller bodies, which indicated a lack of nutrition. It is uncertain the exact year the last remaining Norse left the island but measurements of oxygen isotopes in tooth enamel showed a 1.5 degree Celsius drop in average temperature somewhere between 1100 and 1400. Research indicates that we have several hundred more years of Greenland ice melting before it returns to absolute ice and hardship. Our planet warms and our planet cools. It is unstoppable.

The Sun and clouds!

The biggest object in our solar system is our sun, the most important factor to life on Earth! The sun is the primary driving force of climate, moves weather, ocean currents, evaporation, and provides the energy necessary for life. If we were to have a stronger sun our oceans would boil and life would cease to exist. If our sun were cooler, Earth would freeze and all life on Earth would be gone. The sun is the most overlooked ingredient in climate change for liberals because it doesn't fit their agenda. Orbital variations and changes in energy are emitted from the sun but liberals only speak of this in whispers as to not upset the focus that they feel should be on C02. Solar energy affects our entire way of life because it provides the greatest source of power. When the sun is more energetic, it blasts away at cosmic radiation, resulting in less low-level clouds and therefore our planet reflects less energy back into space. When we experience a weaker sun, more cosmic radiation forms low-level clouds resulting in more energy reflecting back into space. More sun energy=less clouds and less energy into space and making the earth warmer. Less sun energy = more clouds and more energy into space making earth cooler. Our sun drives cosmic radiation forcing changes in our climate. Solar cycles of 11,22, 87, 210, and 1500 years have been found in a variety of different forms of evidence. From ice sheets, ice melting, floods, droughts, lake and seabed sediment; cave deposits, tree rings, fossilized pollen, peat and floating organisms in the Northern and Southern Hemisphere. The vast amount of tangible evidence shows zero correlation between C02 and temperature. There is no link between the past, present or future in regards to C02 and temperature. The main relationship between Earth's climate and the changes that take place are revealed when probing the vast amount of evidence our sun provides. It is the main source of life for Earth and the most powerful celestial object in our solar system. In reality the debate is over in regards to CO2, especially when the worlds premier research center can demonstrate how the sun is the ultimate driver of temperature on Earth. At CERN, the European Organization for Nuclear Research, the one responsible for building the Hadron Collider and inventor the World Wide Web and is home to 8,000 scientists in over 60 countries. CERN is considered the foremost leader of scientific research. The scientists at CERN were able to recreate the Earth's atmosphere, an incredible feat to say the least. Sixty-three scientists, in particular, properly displayed how cosmic rays promote the formation of molecules in Earth's atmosphere, which can grow and seed clouds, providing remarkable insight to the sun's ability to control our climate. Because these scientists were able to grow and seed clouds it showed the cloudier it becomes, the cooler it will be. Since, the sun's magnetic field controls how many cosmic rays reach Earth's atmosphere, this directly correlates to the sun controlling the earth's temperature. Remember, the stronger the sun's magnetic field the more it shields Earth from incoming cosmic rays. Further demonstrating the effect it has on either side of the coin. This points out the incredible magnitude at which the sun is responsible for cloud formation, which results in temperature formation.

, change in cloudiness of planet Earth could account for all the
ıtury warming," according to Australia's best known geologist
.ner, author of *Heaven and Earth*. As he also points out, the IPCC
conv. niently does not bother with cloud formations. Left wing wacko
environmentalists can not simple ignore the effect of cloud formation along
with the biggest and most powerful source of energy in our galaxy because
it doesn't fit their agenda.

O is for "Obtaining" better education for our children

W e can do so much better for the children of America than our current public school system of socialized education. How many times must we fail our own students at the expense of union benefits? Why do we protect rotten teachers who only care about themselves instead of the children? The left wing party has taken over education in America in the name of union domination. Unions certainly aren't looking out for best interest of your child. What they want is job protection, increased pay and no competition from any alternatives that might be available. The longer children remain in America's school systems, the worse off they become. The education system in America has failed miserably and it is time to put the power back into the hands of our nation's students.

Unions, how much control do they really have?

The teachers' union control over children's education is a strict form of socialism. We truly do have a socialized system, yet that's not how liberals want it to come off. Children from 35 other countries are outpacing the United States school system. Unfortunately, the Democrats' agenda, along with the teachers' unions, continue to put a stranglehold on American's education of our children. 50 different unions, including the National Education Association have lined up to repeal the reforms that the

American Federation for Children has put into place for the last decade. Unions see competition as the biggest threat to job security.

The purpose of education is to help young people gain knowledge so that they can succeed later in life. Teachers build a foundation for students to help them learn the necessary skills needed to create the life each child has always dreamed of. My beautiful wife, Amy, is one of those teachers. In my opinion she is the best but that's not what this is about. What it is about is how she provides for her students by giving them her time and energy while making sure they develop as students. She deeply cares how they grow and commands respect in the classroom by demanding that her students try hard and learn. She is one of many great teachers out there; unfortunately there are many bad teachers as well. The union's goal is not about children's success; no they would rather keep their job and maintain high salaries whether or not they perform well in the classroom. Its not about the kids, it's about them.

There is a huge myth that school achievement and more spending have a connection. In fact this is not the case at all. If the amount of school spending were the answer to our education problems, then America's public schools would have yielded the results! Adjusted for inflation, we have doubled the amount of spending per child in the last 30 years and we haven't improved anything. One could make the case that things are actually worse. According to the United States government-spending chart, the federal government spent 70 billion dollars in 2010 on pre-primary through secondary education. 70 billion dollars spent by our federal government and for what? Yet liberals across America continue to yell and scream that we don't spend enough. How much is enough? Every single American knows our government is almost broke, so why all the cries for cuts to our defense system when it's the single most important job for our government to perform!

It's about time we start speaking the truth about our education system. It's not about more money, more money, and more money. All that does is stuff the pockets of the teachers unions. It's about reforming education for our children. It's about competition for school choice. It's about merit-based pay for teachers, rewarding the best teachers for their performance instead of keeping ones job through the backing of powerful unions who are backed by the powerful lawyers associations. It's about allowing parents the opportunity to send their children to the school that best fits their child; whether that's using government coupons to aide parents or allowing for more charter schools to flourish. The point is to break free from the monopoly big government has forced upon us.

We are faced with a public school system that currently graduates only 3/10 students on time. If you are minority things get a lot worse. 1 out of every 2 students won't graduate on time or at all! Estimates show that more young black men are in prison then are in college. If you are a black male you have a 60% chance of ending up in prison if you don't graduate high school and a 72% chance of being unemployed in your 20s. Talk about failure. In cities all across America, the youth are being cheated out of an education. Which means what? It means they will not have a fulfilling life filled with promise and hope. There is a lot of blame to go around but by far the most falls on the shoulders of the selfish, arrogant, bullies of the teachers unions. We all know that unions originally fulfilled a purpose many years ago. Nevertheless, the lure of power and money has caused them to lose their way. The have become hyper-focused on making sure only three things happen: The unions stay in power through large cash infusions, teachers have tenure no matter how pathetic their performance and that school choice is not an option. These all come at the expense of the very people they are supposed to be protecting. Take for example the generous act of philanthropist Robert Thompson. He offered the city of Detroit 200 million dollars to build 15 charter schools. He did this in the name of children and in their best interest. This would have allowed children, especially those coming from very poor families, to send their children to a school where they could flourish! The goal was to have a 90% graduation rate and a 90% college attendance rate. 90% is an ambitious goal for an area that doesn't come close to this figure. Nevertheless he continued with his bold plan of providing an alternative to public schools to the delight of parents throughout Detroit. Michigan's Republican state legislature and Democratic governor approved the charter school option, but Detroit's public school bureaucrats rejected it. The Federation of Teachers destroyed this wonderful project by threatening to strike if the school district accepted this generous proposal from Mr. Thompson. They even tried to paint Mr. Thompson as a racist for helping young black children. I'm not sure how they could get away with that but they tried nonetheless. It is truly unfortunate when the socialistic mob mentality of the teachers unions put their jobs ahead of the hopes and dreams of Detroit's young children. The left never steps up to defend children, especially poor children whose chance at success in life is crushed before they are even 20 years old. Democrats and the liberal teachers unions need to face the fact that they are responsible for ruining the lives of millions of young Americans.

Public schools are ruining the education of our youth and here is one more unfortunate story to back up this point. An easy comparison between America and Europe was shown in John Stossils' book, "Myth's, lies, and downright stupidity." He and his researchers took a look at an above average high school in New Jersey and above average high school in Belgium. It is sad to say but Belgium crushed the United States. Are Belgian kids just born smarter than American kids? Of course not! They have school competition, which produces better teachers and better schools. The report also showed, the longer you stay in American public schools, the worse off students become. (¾ of high school seniors can't identify the purpose of the U.S. House of Representatives) At age 10, the American children who took the international test scored well above the international level. Yet by age 15, America comes in at 25th place! See America has been stuck with a monopoly in our education system. If they don't perform well, then, oh well you are stuck with them. However, in Belgium and in other European schools they have a voucher system that allows for competition. If the school your child is attending is not performing well, they can leave and go somewhere else. It's to the benefit of the student, not the union as it is in America.

If you are a teacher in the New York City school system you can be terrible and it doesn't matter. Unions have created such a roadblock when it comes to firing bad teachers that it's almost impossible to get rid of them. Another example from Stossel's book, showed just how bad it's become. They found in over 200 hundred pages of bureaucracy, just how hard it is to fire bad teachers to make room for good ones. Here's just one example that Stossel and his team found: "It took years to fire a teacher who sent sexually oriented e-mails to "Cutie 101," a 16-year-old student. Joel Klein, chancellor of New York City's public schools said, "He hasn't taught, but we have had to pay him, because that's what's required under the contract." Only after six years of litigation were they able to fire him. In the meantime, they paid the teacher more than $300,000. Klein said he employs dozens of teachers who he's afraid to let near the kids, so he has them sit in what are called rubber rooms. This year he will spend $20 million dollars to warehouse teachers in five rubber rooms. It's an alternative to firing them. In the last four years, only two teachers out of 80,000 were fired for incompetence. Klein's office says, new contracts will make it easier to get rid of sex offenders, but it will still be difficult to fire incompetent teachers.

When Stossel confronted Randi Weingarten, president of the United Federation of Teachers, she said, "They [the NYC school board] just don't want to do the work that's entailed." But the 'work that's entailed' is so onerous that most principals just have just given up, or gotten bad teachers to transfer to another school. They even have a name for it: "the dance of the lemons." That's not how a school should be run and that's not how a business should be run. So what can we do? We obviously need to take power away from the unions. It is a large task and something that can't be dismantled overnight. One thing we can do is shed some light on the vicious and job crushing ways of the Democratic union machine. As Michelle Malkin reported, "Back in May 2008, as he jockeyed with rival Hillary Clinton for Big Labor support, Obama promised to end longstanding federal probes into the Teamsters' mob racket. In 1989, the union was facing federal racketeering charges after Justice Department officials determined it was operating as a "wholly owned subsidiary of organized crime." The Wall Street Journal reported that Obama phoned several Teamsters to convey his vow to begin dismantling the independent federal watchdog overseeing the Teamsters; an Obama spokesman confirmed it." Remember that the teachers union gave 25 million dollars in campaign

of Education at the University of Illinois, making it all the way to "distinguished professor and senior university scholar." Oh just as a side note, he is a friend and campaign contributor to Obama.

Two:

Terrorist teacher number 2 has made the list as one of the worst individuals in our academic institutions. Professor Nicholas De Genova at Columbia Univeristy is another teacher who deserves to be removed from this country and dropped off in the middle of the desert. This man has called for "a million Mogadishus." This of course is in reference to the 1993-downed military mission that left 18 American soldiers dead. He told 3,000 Columbian students, "U.S. flags are the emblems of the invading war machine in Iraq today. They are the emblems of the occupying power. The only true heroes are those who find ways to help defeat the United States military." Those are very strong anti- American sentiments and it would be bad enough if someone overheard him telling his friend these things. Yet he his telling 3,000 of his own students this garbage! Impressionable minds are being manipulated by left wing propaganda. These students are like puppets in a big game called power. By confusing enough minds into thinking the United States is somehow wrong and evil: these radical teachers will indeed find their message to some of these young men and women. He has also expressed his views of Israel in 2002 basically stating that the oppression of Israel is justified by Arab states.

Three:

Many people already know this next terrorists teacher and if you don't, you will now. He is one of the most egregious offenders to the idea of freedom, America's value system and free market principals. Chomsky is the professor of modern languages of linguistics at Massachusetts Institute of Technology since 1955. His most recent book, *Hegemony or Survival,* is as David Horowitz says in his book, *The Professors,* an attack on America as a threat to global survival. As Horowitz again mentions, the Chicago

Tribune says Chomsky is, '"the most cited living author" and ranks right behind Plato and Freud as the most cited of all time. He is revered in anti-American circles and definitely the most influential political mind in academia today. He is also a strident believer in communism, of course. Despite visiting East Asia he never has accepted the fact that communism brutally killed over two million Cambodians because of the communist victories and America's withdrawal. This is an unbelievable trait of far left liberals. If something bad happens that contradicts their belief system, just deny it ever happened. Blaming a bad rice crop is a way of escaping reality. Blaming the United States is a making a conscience effort to bite the hand that feeds you. He believes America is the bad guy and there is no changing his mind. The problem is that he is bent on changing everyone else's mind, especially the young. According to Chomsky, "they (the United States military) have all been either outright war criminals or involved in serious war crimes." His other source of hatred is the subject of Israel. He regards Israel as "an offshore military and technology base for the United States." He is a supporter of holocaust revisionists and dismisses the 9/11 attacks. He remarked that Bill Clinton's attack on a factory in the Sudan (which was an absolute weak response to 2 US embassies that were bombed by Al-Queda) was worse than 9/11. First of all, one person was killed or injured (depending on which source one uses) in the Bill Clinton attack. Second, over 3,000 people were killed in 9/11 at the hands of ruthless, militant Islamic terrorists. He has stated that America is "the world greatest terrorist state" and he only helps to incite the Muslim world be repeating his claims that the United State's liberation of Afghanistan will cause four millions deaths. Despite his efforts to indict the United States of causing genocide, there were over 350 million dollars in food shipments and no genocide. Basically, Chomsky believes the problem is America and it's great to see third world countries fighting back at us. Too bad he doesn't realize that if America were to be destroyed there would be no hope for the defenseless.

He fails to comprehend all the great acts America does for the rest of the world. He purposely discounts the enormous amounts of aid we give to third world countries. The fact that we are the only super power in the history of the world to invade, conquer ruthless totalitarian regimes, help build back the lives of the oppressed people and leave them to be free is completely lost on him. No other country in the history of the world has done that. We give the power back to the local government in hopes that the good people of the country will stay in power. Why won't he and others mention how we are the freest nation on Earth? Every one of these 25,000 terrorist teachers strikes a similar message of hate for America, hatred of Israel, hatred of capitalism, support of Marxism and affiliation with radical Muslims.

The point in mentioning these teachers is twofold. To expose these (25,000 or so) radical teachers for who they really are and to point out the true agenda in America's Universities. Some liberals have figured out that you must rally the youth. You take the topics and spin it in your favor. Young minds are impressionable and you have them for fours years, maybe longer. Combined with the fact that Democrats have planted the idea that you need a college degree to have any kind of success in life goes hand in hand with their plan. College tuitions are absolutely out of control. The plan goes like this: Tell the young children in this world they must get a college degree, best if it comes from an elite university. It doesn't matter that it will cost you 40,000-70,000 dollars a year! Then the indoctrination begins. They have susceptible minds that are concerned with learning, earning a grade to advance, and finding a job to make a living. Students are then exposed to the propaganda of the liberal cause. I really do feel that fighting terrorists and not appeasing them is the most important act Americans can do. The coercion and manipulation of America's youth is right up there as one of the most dangerous dilemmas we face because the liberal agenda is severely damaging America from within. The sad, frustrating part is that no one is there to stop them and no one is there to correct them. Just the other day, a friend of mine went to a teaching seminar. The (so called) acclaimed teacher got up in front of hundreds of teachers and began to explain different ways and methods to teaching. Towards the end of the speech he began with the attacks on using religion (even though my friend is Christian and teaches at a Christian school) and then began the assault on humans destroying the earth. He claimed there is no debate and that the teachers he was addressing need to alert and instruct the children in their classrooms on the dangerous of global warming. Needless to say my friend was furious and thankfully told me all about it. I couldn't believe it. The debate is over? The debate is over in that there is NO global warming and that man has nothing to do with climate change. This was a first hand example with someone trying to instruct a close friend of mine to teach kids a dangerous and completely false subject matter to further the liberal cause. The frightening reality is that these kinds of liberal lies happen everyday in our school system. Teachers are not teaching material based on facts but on agendas. Our children are suffering and so will America in the coming years.

We must spread the word to let people know their children are being brainwashed by Marxist revolutionary ideas. Democrats need puppets to further their cause. They need people to feed into their ideas; in hopes of carrying them to victory come election time. Their ultimate goal is keeping themselves in power for the foreseeable future, but we are fighting back with truth and reality. We are peeling back the layers of manipulation and confusion like an onion to expose their radical ideas for what they truly believe. When the time comes to make a decision on your child's high school education, do your research and choose wisely. When it is time for a decision on college – since inflation on college tuition is over 400% in the last 25 years- maybe college doesn't make sense anymore. If college is the right move, there are a limited amount of options out there that actually embrace values, America and capitalism, but there are a few. Be very careful and remember- Democrats want people they can control and who don't know the facts. Be above them and eliminate their control by seeking the truth, using your morals and seeking the truth. Perhaps these teachers need examples of how great this nation really is.

Here is a beautiful example of how terrorist teachers along with American haters either ignore history or simple don't understand what our founders went through to gain our independence. I'm willing to bet that the radicals inside and out of the country don't even know how the star spangled banner came to be. Because it's truly an amazing, inspiring story that embraces the essence of what it means to be an American. It remembers the remarkable acts of bravery, honor and self-sacrifice to preserve this great nation. It went something like this: Both the British and the Americans had prisoners of war. The men of the colonies sent a representative out to negotiate for the prisoner exchange, a man named Frances Scott Key. They reached a decision to exchange on a one-to-one basis. Frances Scott Key went below the deck of the boat (where the men were being held) and told the men, "Tonight you are free. You will be taken out of your filth and chains." The Admiral of the British went to tell Scott Key one more thing. He said, "we will still honor the prisoner exchange, but after tonight it probably won't matter." Scott Key didn't know what he meant, but the Admiral said, "Tonight we have laid out an ultimatum upon the colonies. Either your people will agree to surrender, lay down the colors of that flag that you love so much, (flying over Fort Henry) or will we will remove Fort Henry from the face of this Earth." Scott Key asked, "Well how do you intend to do such a thing?" The Admiral replied, "look to the horizon. Do you see all those speckled dots? That is the entire British War fleet, which will be arriving in just over 2.5 hours. When we the reach the port the war will be over." Scott Key begged the Admiral to reconsider, stressing that Fort Henry is predominately a non-military fort comprised mainly of men, women and children. The Admiral told him, "We have left them a way out. Do you see that flag, way up over the rampart? We told them that if you lower that flag the shelling of bombs would stop immediately. We will then know that you have surrendered, that the war is over and that you are now under British rule." Francis Scott key then went below deck and told the men what was about to happen. There were hundreds of British ships drawing closer and Francis Scott Key told the men he would shout down and report what was happening as the battle was beginning to unfold. As day had turned to night, the first wave of bombs began to strike. There were so many bomb strikes that it was deafening. Although darkness had taken, the amount of firepower had lit the sky as bombs were bursting away. From the men down below their only concern was, "tell us where the flag is." "Is the flag still flying over the ramparts?" Three hours in to the relentless barrage of bombs the flag was still flying. They could see it by the orange and red sky that was illuminated by the explosions. He kept reporting, "Its sill up! It's not down yet"! The admiral said, "Your people are crazy! Don't they understand that this is an impossible situation"! Francis Scott Key remembered what their leader, George Washington said. "The thing that sets the American Christian apart from all other people in the world is that he would rather die on his feet than die on his knees." Then the Admiral instructed his men to focus all of our guns and that rampart and take that flag down. He told Scott Key, "We don't understand something. Our reconnaissance tells us that, the flag has been hit again and again and we don't understand how it's still flying." The Admiral then said that the next three hours worth of guns would be pointed at that flag. It was unrelenting. The only sound that Scott Key heard with his men was the sound of them praying, asking God, to please keep that flag flying. Sunrise came, and along with it a heavy mist. But the rampart was tall enough that you could see it over the fog. And there stood the flag, in a tattered mess. Still flying just as the men had hoped. Although it was at an odd angle it was still up. Francis Scott Key went on land into Fort Henry and found that the flag had suffered a repetitious amount of direct hits. And each time the flag had fallen, men, fathers, sons had given their life to hold it back up. They knew what it meant to keep that flag flying. Each man came over and gave his life to keep that flag flying. The fallen were removed and replaced each time with another man who gave his life to America to hold that flag. The reason the flag was flying at the odd angle were the patriot's bodies. This gave life to our national anthem:

Oh, say can you see by the dawn's early light
What so proudly we hailed at the twilight's last gleaming?
Whose broad stripes and bright stars thru the perilous fight,
O'er the ramparts we watched were so gallantly streaming?
And the rocket's red glare, the bombs bursting in air,
Gave proof through the night that our flag was still there.
Oh, say does that Star-Spangled Banner yet wave
O'er the land of the free and the home of the brave!

The fight to keep that flag flying and save this great nation from defeat was one of the most heroic, unbelievable accomplishments in American history. The spirit to keep fighting for freedom that our ancestors so proudly displayed is the very essence of what it means to be an American. We will not lie down our arms and give way to appeasement. We will not forget the sacrifices and bravery or those who have gone before us to satisfy some crazed notion of political correctness. We must honor those who have kept us free and maintain our leadership across this globe as the protectors of peace and the enforcers of good will. Today, we have egregious examples of terrorist teachers trying to fight us from within. We can't do anything about it, unless we are aware of the situation we are facing. Many teachers don't embrace the amazing story of how America came to be nor do they support our efforts to stabilize and promote peace throughout the world. So why do they feel they have to unleash their twisted versions of the United States on everyone else? If there are approximately 25,000 of these horrifying people at our universities, doesn't that make you mad! Doesn't that make you want to remove them at once? It sure strikes a cord with me. Inflation has gone up 100% in the last 25 years. Medical care has gone up 218% in this same time period but college tuition has gone up 400% and yet, parents are supposed to pay a fortune to indoctrinate their own children? We must help others become more aware of the threat these teachers pose, understand the dangers they create for our youth and banish them from our schools by putting tighter restrictions on those wishing to become employed as a teacher. They are damaging America from within and they know it. They not only know it, they relish in it. This is their purpose for living and they are instructing the youth with their Marxist, propaganda and pro-terrorists rhetoric.

Origins of socialized education

Our current style of education is the ultimate slap in the face. We have an education system that is chalk full of liberal, progressive teachers and leaders who indoctrinate their students with Marxist rhetoric, while parents are forced to cough up huge sums of money. In short, parents across America are forced to pay for the indoctrination of their sons and daughters.

The current style of public school in America's school system was used a long time ago, before America itself was even established. The Prussian model of education was presented as a component of national planning. This quite frankly makes me a little sick to think about. School administrators were told to churn out as many productive children for the state as possible. Think about it this way: The powerful decision makers of the country enslave their little worker ants by teaching students just enough of one skill to make them productive and useful in their scheme of national economic development. This at its heart is the progressive vision for education. Indoctrination of our youth dates back to the 1650 when compulsory schools were first introduced. Calvin Stowes was an influential voice in leading the United States to adopt Prussian style compulsory schools. As Kevin Williamson stated is his book *The Politically Incorrect Guide to Socialism*, "Regard for public safety makes it right for the government to complete the citizens to do military duty when the country is invaded, the same reason authorizes the government to complete them to provide for the education of their children…a man has no more right to endanger the state by throwing upon it a family of ignorant and vicious children, than he has to give admission to the spies of an invading army."

The cause to make the children slaves of the state has gone on for a long time and continues today. Take for example President Obama's talk that he gave to school children describing in detail how they can help serve the needs of the state. He made sure to stress his agenda of healthcare, jobs, racial discrimination, and environmental concerns during his talk, of course. He said, "You'll need the insights and critical thinking skills you gain in history and social studies to fight poverty and homelessness, crime and discrimination and make our nation fairer and freer. We need every single one of you to develop your talents, skills and intellect so you can help solve our most difficult problems." The message itself does not sound all that bad. However, when you consider that the message is coming from a socialist president who views the education system as a means of control then it becomes a political ploy. Obama went on to say, "If you don't do that-if you quit on school- you're not just quitting on yourself, you're quitting on your country." Some parents were rightly upset that his speech was broadcasted into all of the nation's government run schools and resembled political indoctrination. Others on the left were not surprised at all. As one writer of a left wing website, Daily Kos wrote, "If your kids are in school, they're already living that agenda." Just in case people didn't quite grasp his comments, he headlined his post, "Public Schools Are Socialist." Writer Daniel Reneau at *Helium*, prosed the question, "Like public schools? Then say, 'thank you socialism!'" We know the educators and administrators of the system like the ways their system works. And why is that? Because there is no competition! The government provides them with salaries and benefits greater than the private sector. Besides which, it is extremely hard to be fired from public schools no matter how hard you try. I can see why it's a pretty comfortable position to be in.

Public schools in the poor black communities are not good at all. One doesn't have to think very hard to wonder why. There is one school in each district. Each child must attend the school closest to their residence, forcing uniformity throughout each area. If you are from a lousy school district, then what do you do? If you can't afford to go to private school you have 2 choices. Struggle on or simply quit. Since you can't go to another school you are forced into this dilemma. As Williamson says, "This also means that the character of your school is dependent upon the residential community. So the schools are from within each district and the composition of pupils, financing of each school and quality of education are dependent upon the values of the community, wealth and tax base of each geographical area."

Newton Bateman who called for a socialist model of mandatory schooling of education wrote, "(education) was too important to be left to the marketplace, a good that it "cannot be left to the caprices and contingencies of individuals." As Obama said, right of "eminent domain" of over the "hearts and minds and bodies" of the nations children in support of his case. Bateman went further in his cause and tried to ban all private schools in 1922, stating the need for uniform education to make good citizens and productive workers. Its sounds like he wants little ants, each doing their job according to their skill for the betterment of the queen, or nanny state. William Seawell, a professor at the University of Virginia argued, "State schools unlike private schools promote civic rather than individual pursuits...creating citizens for the good of society...each child belongs to the state." They really do want to control your every move. The theme again and again is> control and money v. freedom.

The education system in America is in a crisis just like our financial situation and reform cannot come soon enough. One sign of hope has come from the inner circles of Governor Rick Perry, from the great state of Texas. Brooke Rollins, the President of Texas Public Policy Foundation, (a free market research group aligned with Perry) put forth a proposal to turn the education policies of Texas upside down. The first major overhaul would be to put the money back in the hands of the consumer. Instead of the money going straight to public colleges and universities, some of the money would go into the palms of students in the form of grants. Instead of administrators having all the power, the consumers would get that power back. This would create competition not only to improve the quality of the school but also to reduce price increases that have gone up drastically in the last 25 years. The proposal has already been put forth but was shot down by educational elites because of their unwillingness to give up the power they have over the consumer. The other proposal was dubbed, "outcomes-based funding." The premise is to secure a relationship between the amounts of money a school receives to the number of students each school graduates. I know you must be thinking, that will just increase the likelihood of teachers altering grads, right? Not with this plan. There would be an exiting exam that each student would take before graduating. It would not affect whether or not they received their diploma, but the test would provide concrete data showing how much learning is actually taking place. Of course, the establishment has successfully shot down this proposal as well, since it's seen as a threat to their jobs instead of a way to evaluate student's progress. The need to make teachers more accountable has never been more apparent that it is today. Data shows that the longer a child stays in school the less he or she is learning. Just 5 years can make a huge difference. Remember, by age ten, children in America score fairly well on international tests, but by age fifteen, their test scores drop all the way down to twenty-fifth in the world.

Teachers are responsible for the growth of each student's academic growth. However, when we can't see that growth or it is masked by teacher manipulation then you are failing the student. Parents need to clearly see the work of their child to know if they indeed comprehending the material. If schools are not held responsible for their inability to teach children in a productive manner then how can our children succeed further down the road in life? The elucidation of how well each school functions must be apparent.

Competition can come in the form of school choice through voucher programs as well as charter schools. Parents have a right to send their child wherever they want to send them. It should not be decided by what street you live in which ultimately defines what kind of shot your child has at leading a nice life. If you are unlucky and are stuck with a terrible school system why is that your only choice? Competition creates improvement, which in the end only helps your child. What liberals don't understand is that our current system of socialized education is the detriment of each and every single child.

M is for "Misleading" Media

As Fred Barnes noted even in 2004, "the argument over whether the national press is dominated by liberals is over. In 1971, they were 53 percent liberal, 17 percent conservative. A 1985 poll of 3,200 reporters found them to be self-identified as 55 percent liberal, 17 percent conservative." Although that was the 70's and 80's, the discrepancy has actually gotten worse. Barnes continues, "In 1996, another survey of Washington journalists pegged the breakdown as 61 percent liberal, 9 percent conservative. Now, the new study by the Pew Research Center for the People and the Press found the national media to be 34 percent liberal and 7 percent conservative. Over 40-plus years, the only thing that's changed in the medias politics is that many national journalists have now cleverly decided to call themselves moderates." Unfortunately for the American people, the idea of bipartisan political reporting has gone by the wayside and we have been left with a media that's not only more liberal, but hides the fact that they lean far left and pretend they reside in the middle. Barnes further explains that "the proportion of liberals to conservatives in the press, either 3-to-1 or 4-to-1, has stayed the same. That liberals are dominant is now beyond dispute." One would think that the freest nation on earth would have unbiased, fair reporting across the all segments of the political spectrum. Yet, the research shows how the media can report whatever they want, without repercussion, to the detriment of the American people.

Clear differences in the way the Media reports

Remember how nasty the liberal media was towards President Bush? It was blatant evidence of just how far liberals were willing to go in order to paint him as the worst president in history. All the media did was to back liberals every opportunity they were given. It was like, once one person took off the gloves, the liberal mob mentality started swinging and boundaries were crossed. The more they bashed him the more the media's false rhetoric became second nature. Americans began to think President Bush really was a hate-filled, moron. Now think for one second about the media's beloved- Obama. Has there ever been a media more in love, more impressed with an under qualified community organizer who is allowed to rewrite is own version of history? NO! Therefore we need to take a step back. Lets do a side-by-side comparison between then President Bush and now dictator Obama.

What if George W. Bush had doubled the national debt in one year? What if George W. Bush had then proposed to double the debt again within 10 years, would you still think he knows what is best for the country? What if George W. Bush had sided with Mexico in suing the United States so that illegal immigration could continue? Wouldn't that be enough to question if this president was really on the side of the United States? Would it have been okay for George W. Bush to bow to all the leaders of other countries- even when that is completely contrary to any action the president of the United States of America has ever done? Would you have been completely embarrassed if George W. Bush had said in front of a Mexican crowd how great the celebration of "Cinco de cuartro" was, instead of "Cinco de Mayo." Would you have told him, brush up on your Spanish before you further embarrass yourself? What If George W. Bush put 87,000 workers out of work by arbitrarily placing a moratorium on offshore oil drilling, even though that company had an extremely high safety record, but did so because of pressure from his special interest groups? What if George W. Bush was unable to make it through a press conference without a teleprompter? Wouldn't you call this guy a moron? What if George W. Bush had allowed Air Force One and jet fighters to intentionally fly very low over Manhattan causing fear and panic among the people below them? Would you regard him as brainless and inconsiderate? What if George W. Bush measured himself such an amazing speaker, that he gave the Queen of England an ipod containing brilliant oratory remarks that he himself gave? Wouldn't you think this guy's head must be so large, that it's amazing he doesn't struggle going through doorways? What if George W. Bush walked into a company and scrapped their retirement plan and then handed unions the majority ownership of said company? Would you think this guy is acting more like the president of Russia? What if George W. Bush made fun of the Special Olympics? Wouldn't that make you angry? What if George W. Bush, upon visiting Austria, referenced the "Austrian language," of which does not exist? Would it cause you to stop and think, maybe he really isn't all that worldly. What George W. Bush had insisted that there really are 57 states in America? Would you have called him an idiot? What if George W. Bush burned 9,000 gallons of jet fuel to plant a single tree on Earth day? Would you say that's a little hypocritical? What if George W. Bush created positions out of thin air to allow 32 separate Czars to report directly to him, bypassing the House and Senate? Wouldn't you call him a dictator? What if George W. Bush, without any constitutional authority, fired a CEO of a major corporation? Wouldn't you be upset and consider him to be a president who feels he is above the law?

The point is, all those ridiculous statements and actions were said and done by Obama and not Bush. And yet we still find Obama, protected by the liberal media bent painting him in the best light possible. They've created quite a cushy cocoon that allows him to say or do whatever he wants. A good analogy might go something like this: Obama is like a basketball player who is told by everyone how good he is (speeches). They constantly tell him how beautifully he plays the game (decisions). That during times of uncertainly, when his team is trailing that he remains calm (calls for more press conferences). We are then told how amazing he is at finding open teammates by distributing the ball (goodies, handouts, welfare state). Then upon further examination, we come to find out he's a lousy player, terrible leader on the court, blames all his teammates and never himself, and constantly cries about not getting the ball. Then after the game, in which he did nothing to help his team, the media gushes over him in admiration for what a beautiful game he played. I never in my life thought I would see such awestruck wonder for the most anti-American, anti-freedom, pro big government, lying, overrated, teleprompt reading president. Since 89% of the media are liberal, Obama gets to say whatever he wants without repercussion. Our media is only concerned with praising "their guy" and hurting the other side.

Who can you trust?

There is a reason conservatives have a stronger voice now more than ever. We are closer to leveling the playing field. Fox News – the most widely watched political channel is actually balanced and might lean slightly to the right. Talk radio: The lineup of Bill Bennett, Mike Gallagher, Glenn Beck, Dennis Prager, Rush Limbaugh, Michael Medved and Hugh Hewitt and Sean Hannity has changed American politics. These radio hosts provide the most accurate, informative, substantive material that one could ever hope to find. Everyday their shows consist of clear, concise information that has helped shaped the minds of millions and millions of listeners. They allow for civil discourse from both sides. It is the saving grace for conservatives, so of course liberals are trying to take it away by instituting the fairness doctrine. This would allow big government to control the amount of content each side of the isle could use. Since liberal talk radio is nonexistent, take a guess at which side would be hurt? You got it, the Republican Party. 50% of the content would have to be devoted to liberalism, perhaps forcing the shutdown of talk radio. Nothing about this liberal proposal would be fair, but that hasn't stopped them from trying.

A perfect example of media manipulation by liberals

The liberal media's ability to spin the truth, in the face of the largest amount of evidence stating the contrary is well...purposeful. What if we had a glaring example of left wing media propaganda? One might laugh and say we get that every night! True, but this particular media offense has lead to the staying power of Marxist revolutionary ideas. First let us take a step back:

Imagine a warrior, backed by the leaders of his country, was said to be the end all be all. Every news outlet adorned him, praised him, and told him how remarkable he was in freeing his people. His legendary status spread like wild fire and his tales of bravery, honor inspiration stretched across the globe. He led his troops through battle, conquered invading armies, liberated his people and overall was the face of his party. The media hailed him as one of the great icons in world history. You might think to yourself, what an amazing person! Now, what if we were fortunate enough to have first hand detailed accounts from those who served under this warrior stating facts contrary to every media report? What if you came to find out that this so called warrior murdered tens of thousands of innocent people, called for the death of the United States, plotted a terrorist attack that would have been larger than 9/11 (was thankfully stopped by the FBI), repeatedly called for the end of individualism and was quoted in the London Daily Worker saying, "If nuclear missiles had remained we would have used them against the very heart of America, including New York City." Without revealing who this was, so as to not cloud your judgment, I believe any reasonable person would conclude that the murdering of one innocent person let alone tens of thousands would lead you to condemn him. When he called for nuclear missiles to be used on the United States you would conclude that he is a horrible, crazy terrorist. He was quoted as saying, "a revolutionary must become a cold killing machine motivated by pure hate." This man was Che Guevara.

Side by side comparisons are often helpful and I can think of no better way to illustrate my point than by showing how the media lies to fit their agenda.

Media reports: He displayed outrageous bravery and skill on the battlefield. Truth: Che admits to knowing, "absolutely nothing" on military strategy. Also a bullet did pierce his chin and exit his temple, just missing his brain from his own pistol!

ɔrts: Che in battle- 1,000 killed in 5-day battle

ital casualties on both sides did not exceed 5 people.

Media reports: Eyewitness and invaluable resources are discarded by the media an completely unimportant.
Truth: The totalitarian propaganda machine led by Castro simple made up history and of course the media believes what Castro wrote and not eyewitnesses.

Media reports: Reporters acted as though everything was great down in Cuba. They were impressed that children were vaccinated and food was evenly distributed.
Truth: Cuba officially declares itself a Marxist, Leninist state, sent people to the firing squads, was set up by the East Germany STASI, had secret police spying on citizens at every corner looking for counter revolutionary people.

Media Reports: Reporters and journalists fawn over the man, writing how impressive he was on his visit to NYC.
Truth: The New York Police Department uncovered a plot by Che to blow up the Statue of Liberty, Liberty Bell and the Washington Monument.

Media Reports: Time magazine placed him among "The heroes and Icons of the Century"
Truth: Quotes from the man himself: "We will bring the war to imperialist enemies'very home, to his places of work and recreation" – from his message to the Tri-continental conference in 1967. "We must never give him a minute of peace or tranquility. This is a total war to the death. We'll attack him wherever we find him. The imperialist enemy must feel like a hunted animal wherever he moves. This we'll destroy him!" Who is the enemy? "The great enemy of mankind: the United States of America!"

Remember the horrible 2004 Madrid subway blasts? Che's Cuban agents had planned to set off 5 times that in a terrorists plot targeting

Macy's, Gimbel's, Bloomingdale's, and Manhattan's Grand Central Terminal with 500 kilo's of TNT the day after thanksgiving in 1962. This guy was Bin Laden before there was a Bin Laden. And for some sick, twisted, idiotic reason he his hailed as one of the greatest people of the 21st Century? Don't believe everything you read and hear in the media. While the liberal media was busy gushing over what an impressive, amazing person this terrorist was, he was busy trying to blow them up. Keep your eyes open and remember the liberal media looks for ways to suppress freedom of thought, opinion and ideas.

Hidden Agenda's – never more apparent than now

One of the hottest topics of conversation these days is the agenda to destroy the Tea Party. It is the most vile, blatant abuse of media bias that I've ever witnessed. Liberals call for civility and all they do is bash Republicans. The liberal media has no clue what the Tea Party is all about. Tea Party members are made up of everyday, hardworking people who deeply care about America. The talking heads on television are hate- filled, frustrated simpletons, who will say or do anything to attack Republicans. Journalism is supposed to take an objective view of the issues and report them in a factual manner. However, that is not the case when we run into the likes of the following offenders of media reporting. Let's take a look at a few examples:

1. One of the worst offenders of media bias Chris Matthews. This guy is so nasty we could fill a whole book worth of crazy, offensive, false remarks that its hard to just pick a few. Every single day you find numerous examples of nonsensical waste coming from his mouth. His latest garbage was, "The Tea Party is terrorizing this country with the debt ceiling. When responding to comments from other liberal bashers, he said, "I agree, its terrorism." More from Matthews, "the GOP has become the Wahhabis of American government, willing to risk bringing down the whole country in the service of their anti-tax ideology."

2. Other comments on the Tea Party come from Paul Krugman, "Republicans have, in effect, taken America hostage."

3. New York Times columnist Thomas Friedman said, "If sane Republicans do not stand stand up to this Hezbollah faction in their midst, the Tea Party will send the GOP on a suicide mission."

4. Maureen Dowd compared the Tea Partiers to "budget slashers, cannibals and vampires. These people are so stupid, so mislead and so completely naïve. They are willing to say those comments along with about 100 more for an issue that is so small, that it becomes almost incomprehensible."

Tea Partiers are calling for debt cuts without tax increases. What is wrong with that! Democrats spend like drunken sailors, destroy the value of the dollar and then have the nerve to say that Tea Partiers are like terrorists. She is comparing country loving, normal American citizens to Hezbollah? A terrorist network, which happens to be one of the worst on the face of the earth? The Tea Party people are bringing sanity and solutions back to politics. They are telling our politicians to stop ruining our country. Stop spending, stop appeasing terrorists, stop taking away our rights, stop socialized medicine, stop centralized planning, stop ruining our children's education, stop cap and trade, stop lying to us about climate change, stop forcing us to use energy that doesn't help us. And then nasty, name calling liberals have the audacity to say we Tea Partiers are the terrorists. Why wouldn't they make those nasty comments about all those Occupy Wall Street protestors? It is absolutely incredible that they defend the occupiers of Wall Street that rape, beat people up, cause fights with police, defecate on cars, threaten police, support Socialism and Communism and in general are a disgusting representation of human beings. Why not mention how horrible these people are? No, they won't because our mainstream media only looks out only for the liberal side of America. Occupy Wall Street is about liberalism seeping into the cracks of society to engulf any and all who are uneducated enough to know any better. I believe the crazy liberals in the media and around the United

States are in need of some serious reality checks. I never realized how corrupt our media can be, until I ventured into politics. One would think that the freest country on Earth would have a fair and objective medium. Alas, its not so. Thank God for talk radio and the internet. These outlets of freedom must remain so, to the benefit of every American.

This brings us to perhaps the most irritating, politically corrupt group in the last century. It's a liberal organization, supported by Obama and his administration. I'm talking about the ASSociation of Community Organization for Reform Now, known as ACORN. This group of left wing radicals has gotten away with more corruption and manipulation than anyone could imagine. Yet the media says nothing. We must address two blatantly dishonest programs designed by ACORN that perfectly illustrate the corruption that permeates their organization and which of course, is tied to the Democratic Party.

We can all remember the hard times in 2008, as the subprime mortgage crash ruined lives, crushed pensions and saw foreclosures pop up like clovers after a fresh rain. ACORN was explicitly involved and played a strong role in grinding the economy to a halt. They lobbied legislators and pressured banks to make certain that any person regardless of income; assets or credit worthiness received a loan. Unconcerned with the consequences to follow they became wonderful at pressuring banks to provide subprime loans while knowing full well that defaults were soon to follow. These loans eventually became the toxic ones that were bundled by mortgage giants that ignited the subprime meltdown. The second egregious act that ACORN (but there certainly are many more) actively partakes in, is the rampant voter fraud in connection with the Democratic Party. Frankly, I've never seen anything like it and I can't believe they continue to operate. The amount of fraudulent activity is staggering. *Here are just a few examples* that the FBI found in direct connection to this ridiculous liberal organization.

1998 Arkansas – A contractor connected to ACORN with Project Vote (the name used for voter fraud) was arrested for falsifying 400 voter registration cards. They should cease to exist after this obvious violation of voter fraud alone.

2004 Colorado- ACORN employee admits to forging and registering three of her friends to vote 40 times!

2005 Virginia – The Virginia State Board of Elections reprimanded Project Vote and ACORN for the number of faulty votes they registered. An audit revealed 83% of the sampled registrations were rejected for being fraudulent!

2008 Pennsylvania – State election officials had to throw out 57,435 voter registrations of which the majority was submitted by ACORN!

2008 Texas – In Harris County 10,000 ACORN submitted registrations were invalid. They contained fraudulent addresses and fake personal information.

2008 Ohio – ACORN activists gave Ohio residents' cash and cigarettes in exchange for filling out voter registration cards. One man claimed he signed up on 72 cards. What!

2009 Florida – The Florida Department of Law Enforcement and the state attorney's office found 197 of 260 applications had personal ID information that did not match any living person!

It goes on and on with this organization. Unfortunately, that was just the tip of the iceberg. The sad and disgusting thing is that they still continue to operate and have 75 organizations operating in 38 states across America, as well as offices in Canada, Mexico and Peru. Our only hope is that the FBI continues to arrest and prevent this dirty branch of Democratic Party from getting away with any more voter fraud. The FBI is on record as stating that ACORN is working for the Democratic Party. There should be not doubt left in anyone's mind that liberals and democrats try to cheat the political system. It is bad enough that they ram policies through that the American people don't want. But it is even worse that they cheat like crazy to get incompetent liberal politicians elected.

All the while, the media just looks the other way. It is truly amazing what liberals can get away with. Then again, protecting voter fraud is not too hard if the media refuses to report it.

Closing:

We were so fortunate to have won our independence from Britain, who in the 18th Century was the clear-cut, number one superpower on earth. The simple farmers, countrymen and pioneers of the United States refused to live under the oppression of English rule. Against insurmountable odds, citizens of the 13 colonies united as one country and defeated the greatest army on earth. It was truly amazing how we snatched victory from the jaws of defeat time and time again during our battles against the Brits. It's obvious why we must reference the most significant war in American history. The Revolutionary War was fought because freedom was slowly but surely being taken from those hard working farmers each year. They made the arduous journey across the Atlantic for freedom of religion and the hope of one day owning their own land. The promise of religious freedom and property rights became such enormous incentives that the people couldn't resist, even if it meant becoming an indentured servant for a number of years. Many did indeed, spend years in toil, but to them it was well worth it. Once these newly formed colonialist became established, the overreach of England's government continued to plague them as they sought freedom from excessive taxes and governmental control by the English monarchy. In their strife for freedom came the most valuable piece document every created for the benefit of mankind, the constitution of 1787. Our founding fathers crafted the most enduring document for freedom the world has ever seen. It has proven to be the greatest blueprint on how to build a nation for the betterment of its citizens and not the government. By providing the people with a government divided in its powers of the executive, legislative and judicial branches, it allowed for the correct balance of government authority. The creation of one currency, one market, one army the ideas of religious freedom and property ownership really allowed the citizens to thrive and live a meaningful life free from an overextended government that has plagued every other nation on earth. In the end our founding fathers decided they had had enough of England's governmental control and chose freedom.

The suppression of freedom is taking place now more than ever but not at the hands of a foreign governmental control, like we endured with the Brits. The loss of freedom is happening in an eye-opening fashion at the behest of big government liberalism here in America right now! As Dennis Prager so rightly points out, "The bigger the government, the smaller the citizen." Government must stay out of our way so that we are free to flourish in the greatest economy ever created. Today we are finding freedom stripped from us throughout each segment of our lives. Each year the chains of bondage become tighter around our wrists without us ever being the wiser. These barriers to freedom are fortified through three principal ideologies: the monopolistic rule of big government, the destructive nature of liberalism and the ever-present threat of Islamic extremists. Radicals continue to plot and infiltrate our society, to slowly but surely gain the upper hand in forcing us to either convert to Islam or face elimination. Yet, our liberal leaders only appease them by making excuses, refusing to call them radical Muslims and handcuff our military by eliminating interrogation techniques. Our current liberal government of the United States wants to dictate our health care options by telling us when or if we receive the care we need. Our dollar is being devalued every day by the relentless campaign of quantitative easing to allow liberals to hand out more goodies, further bankrupting our economy. Energy options are being taken away by powerful government mandates telling us how much and what kind of energy we can use. Greenwashing is being pushed down our throat in name of fake global warming by the liberal environmentalists. Our children are forced to listen to Marxist terrorist teachers in our Universities while families cough up hundreds of thousands of dollars for their Marxist rhetoric. American children are stuck in a school system based off of socialism without any choice or competition if they do not have the economic means for private schooling. In the end the American people are left with the mess of figuring out these most important issues all while dealing with a corrupt media bent of portraying every liberal agenda in the proper light.

We can liken these political issues to rose garden. When gardens are cultivated in the right way, they produce roses to the betterment of all, like common sense proposals put forth by free thinking conservatives. But they also produce thorns, which hurt us every time we pick them. Those thorns are the democratic liberal policies, which only serve to hurt the American people in the end. Rose gardens can also contain irritable insects, which cause damage to the beautiful roses by biting and chewing holes in the rose buds. These insects are akin to our mainstream media. The mainstream media only creates havoc by taking bites out of those beautiful roses. When the gardener finally realizes the damage that's being done to his roses, he doesn't just give up. No! He finds out the truth and eradicates those nasty little bugs. That is what we must do my friends, find the truth.

Liberalism has only succeeded in producing only obstacles to freedom. If you had to remember just three, remember these: the Keynesian belief system of spending oneself into prosperity is extremely childish and the biggest reason why empires fall. The appeasement of terrorists is black eye number two in the crumbling of a great society as liberalism goes out of way to help those that want to hurt us. Main obstacle number three is the population reduction supported so fervently by liberals in order to "save the planet." These are parts E, F, and D in the acronym F.R.E.E.D.O.M and the most dangerous of all.

We common sense conservatives can take it no more! Knowledge is power and knowing the truth can lead you to freedom. We strive for Freedom from a government that seeks to control our every move. We plead for a government that listens to us by getting out of our way! We are asking for less government and more freedom, less control over the individual, which will allow us to succeed without government holding us back. Less regulation and more private sector growth, less government interference on prices and more small business growth, less appeasement of terrorists and more pride in America, less government mandated healthcare and more free market solutions, less manipulation of our energy, more drilling of our own natural resources, less preaching of socialism and more implementation of capitalism.

We are fighting to remain the freest nation on Earth. As this fight continues we must stand firm against radicals, appeasement, big government, liberalism and a biased media. Yet, through awareness and understanding we have a chance to overcome these barriers by embracing and supporting the value of individual freedom, while calling upon others to do the same. Your eyes have now been opened to the coercive nature of government. You are free to make the choice for yourself. Continue to let the government wipe your nose until there is nothing left or rise up and live for yourself. You are free to remove the chains of captivity and find freedom. You only get one shot at your life. You can choose to live under government control or embrace the freedom of the individual. Time's a wasting, your move.

Bonus Section: Clear difference between liberals and conservatives

Obama's election to the presidency has been rough on the American people. American's are out of jobs and hurting with unemployment hanging around 8.2% with real unemployment around 15-16%. The Obama administration has failed to deal with a nuclear Iran, removed the ability of our troops to get tactical information from captured terrorists, continue to spend our dollar into nothing, refuse to drill for our own natural resources, continue the promotion of fake global warming, continue the support of teachers unions instead of actively helping our children and are backed by a liberal media that never acknowledges the toxic polices that liberalism creates.

The greatest outcome of the 2008 elections was the first hand example of why liberal policies don't work. It has been sort of a mixed blessing for me. The good part was that it fired me up. I had to know more about politics and I got to the bottom of our countries core issues. The bad part was of course, living with the unfortunate results of misguided liberal policies. Now that I've come to see what both sides stand for, it's really quite clear once you put all the political rhetoric aside. Below in the bonus section, you will see a shorthand version of each party's belief system, so that you can refer to them when sifting through the rhetorical garbage coming from our politicians. The following notes simply describe what each side feels is the best path for the country. To those that feel there is no difference between each party, one can see quite clearly, the path each party would like to take the American people.

Democrat's belief system:
Themes: welfare state, taxing the rich, equality, bigger government, control of people

The foremost idea built into the belief system of liberals is this> **equality.** As Churchill so rightly said, "the inherent vice of capitalism is the unequal sharing of blessing. The inherent vice of socialism is the equal sharing of misery." The fact that the majority of people in Venezuela have an equal share of poor electricity is a good thing to liberals. If a country provides free healthcare, it doesn't really matter that the quality of health care is dreadful throughout the country. What matters is that everyone has something. The idea that things aren't fair is an idea so ingrained into the minds of liberals that it's inconceivable for a country as strong as the United States to not *make* things equal. That's where the role of government comes into play for liberals.

Not good v. evil but rich v. poor. Evil is the root cause of problems in this world according to liberals. They are certain that rich people exploit and manipulate the poor because they have power over others. This is an injustice according to the left. Liberals do not view people as evil, because it is much easier to view them as poor and therefore it's justifiable when people commit crimes. Liberals also believe it is permissible when they riot, storm government buildings and set businesses on fire because they are poor. This means you are making morality take a back seat to equality. The rich need to suffer because they take advantage of the poor. However, this problem has occurred time and time again throughout the ages of history and continues into the present. Life is not free and you can't provide everything to everyone. If that were the case life would be more like a utopian society. I know that's what liberals strive for but me show an instance in human history when giving all the people whatever they want has worked! You can't provide such an instance because the answer is never.

A bigger government provides more compassion for the people. Liberals are concerned with feelings and emotion more the conservatives. This one is hard to explain, because it's counterintuitive. Liberals want the government to take care of the people in everyway possible but this takes away from neighbor helping neighbor. If you want the government provide that food or water or clothing, then you've taken away the act of charity from your fellow American. America is the most charitable nation on earth mainly because of few remaining free market principles we are still embrace. Which only strengthens the reason why Americans are much more generous and giving of their time than any other nation on earth> because we are not a socialist country yet. The government cannot and should not provide every little thing for every single person in America. First of all, the old expression that money does not grow on trees is perfectly applicable in this situation. Second, the government cannot provide for each individual because our society would cease to exist in about 1 month. It is not government's job to live your life.

Liberals believe state control over the economy is a good thing. I really believe in my heart that liberals get overwhelmed. That is to say, they are overwhelmed with all the activities that take place everyday. It is too much for them to handle. Everyday problems are too big for each individual so let the government take over. For them it's better to give up freedom, but to be taken care of. Government loves control and a government cannot control the economy without first controlling the people, as former President Reagan so beautifully said.

Welfare state is king to them because it incorporates every ideal they have about human beings. Liberals feel welfare provides compassion, helps the poor, makes people feel good even if they didn't do anything, and takes care of those who aren't able enough to take care of themselves. In some cases, yes, the government should take care of people. For instance those who are mentally challenged should be taken care of by the state. However, in most instances welfare creates slaves to the state. People count on liberals to take care of them and in return they provide Democrats with votes. To top it off, the welfare state not only fills the void in the lives of those struggling, but it also makes the politicians themselves feel a greater sense of self worth for providing that "free lunch." It is time for Americas on the left to remember the core principals that our founders provided for us. The notion being, that everyone should have an equal opportunity. For liberals they have twisted that beautiful concept into, not equal opportunity, but an equal outcome. That is where they fail to see the difference between the greatness of America, which for them turns into disdain for this great nation. Ultimately, liberals are only left with contempt.

Conservatives belief system:

Smaller government means more individual freedom. **Get out of our way!** When government is forced to take a back seat to the individual, the economy is free to flourish. Think about it this way: government does not make money, right? Government only takes money. If the word tax, which by its very nature means to take away, doesn't that reduce the incentive to work and produce? We work hard for our money and I believe it's safe to say, we all want to keep our hard-earned money. The government wants you to work, so that it can tax you and take your money away from you. Then politicians get to spend it on programs you may or may not agree with. The more tax revenue Washington D.C. collects, the happier big government becomes. It gets to expand! The more you are taxed the less time and money you have. Do you see where I'm going here with this one? You start to become a slave to the state. It is even more frustrating when you have a government that is bent on spending more than it has and prints more than is humanly possible. A bigger government creates its own agenda, were the people become less important. When the government is smaller, people get to steer the direction and movement of the country in a way they see fit.

Bigger government always leads to bigger corruption. A bigger government means more control over the individual. It also means manufacturing the people to put them in slots designed for them to be as productive as they can be for growth of the nanny state. The state says, put in certain amount of hours per week and you will get benefits, pensions, time off, vacations and leisure time with which you can use to enjoy your life. What these people can't see is that you become government's property. You are told when and for how much you will work. It is called government manipulation- it is Orwellian and sickening. It reduces your life to some trivial existence in which you are played on strings like a helpless puppet until your existence ends and someone else comes to take your place. This is actually hard to think about. It is anti human and the people stuck in it can't see their way out of it. Think about the great evils of the world. Those that have murdered in the name of the nanny state- Hitler and the nazis, Stalin and Mao just to name a few. They were responsible for more innocents being murdered in the 20th century than any other group in the world. It is like a bug flying to the neon light that will eventually zap him. The liberals of America are just like the bugs. They are floating along and about to be zapped. As Lenin so grossly put it, "Western companies will vie with one another to sell us the rope by which we will hang them."

Big business and big government go together. Big business, in fact, is way more in line with socialism and liberalism than with conservative principals. Big business and big government both have their corruption except big business has to answer to the police while big government answers to no one. As we've seen when government's reach becomes too long, they have power over their citizens. Look at Russia and how many people have been sent to the Siberian prisons for not going along with the state's agenda. Big government becomes like an out of control train. If you are on it, you are stuck. If you go against it, you are thrown off the train never and never heard from again. Big government is dark and dangerous and yet liberals have placed their trust in the government, not only take care of them but to provide a life of luxury as well. When money runs out, as it always does, their benefits and goodies from the state must eventually go away. Then the mob becomes angry and fights for what they see as rightfully theirs. It is sad and really shows how helpless people become when the government overreaches its hand into society.

Good v. evil does exist. There are examples abound where you can find evil in this world. Those who kill in the name of religion, land, power and money provide us with all too many sad stories. There is definitely evil in this world and it is not because that country or person happens to be poor. Take radical Muslim extremists. They are not killing innocent people all over the world because of poverty. They are killing in the name of religion.

They are killing to take over land they believe is rightfully theirs. To say only rich v. poor exists is to say that no wealthy person has ever killed or hurt people, which we know to be false.

Control over ones self. Conservatives want to be free. We want to control our own destiny. We don't want bureaucrats telling us when, where and how to live our lives. We don't want to be puppets of the state. Instead, we want to be free to make our own way in life. This country began in the name of freedom. Freedom to live out our lives the way we see fit. Freedom to speak when we want to speak; Freedom to write what one wants to write; Freedom to bear arms if we need to; Freedom from unreasonable search and seizures; Freedom to have due process of law- when government's role is limited the individual is free to flourish.

References:

1. Barnes, F. (2004, May). Liberal Media Evidence. *The Weekly Standard*.

2. Bryce, Robert. Power: *The Myths of "Green" Energy and the Real Fuels of the Future*. New York: Public Affairs, 2010. Print.

3. Beck, Glenn. BROKE: *The Plan to Restore Our Trust, Truth and Treasure*. New York: Mercury Radio Arts, Inc., 2010.

4. Bennett, William J and Leibsohn, Seth. The Fight of Our Lives: *Knowing the Enemy, Speaking the Truth and Choosing to Win the War Against Radical Islam*. Nashville Tennessee: Thomas Nelson Inc., 2011.

5. Delingpole, J. (2011, October). *The London Telegraph*.

6. Economics. (2011, March 2nd). *The Wall Street Journal* (Eastern ed.), p.?

7. Ferguson, A. (2011, September). Perry and the Profs. *The Weekly Standard*, 12-14.

8. Ferguson, Charles D. Nuclear Energy: *What Everyone Needs To Know*. New York: Oxford University Press, 2011.

9. Ferguson, Niall. Civilization: *The West and the Rest*. New York: The Penguin Group Inc., 2011.

10. Friedman, George. The Next 100 Years: *A Forecast for the 21st Century*. New York: The Doubleday Publishing Group, 2009.

11. Fontova, Humberto. Exposing The Real Che Guevara: *And the Useful Idiots who Idolize Him*. New York: Penguin Group Inc., 2007.

12. Gonzalez, Guillermo and Richards, Jay W. The Privileged Planet: *How Our Place in the Cosmos is Designed for Discovery*. Washington D.C: Regnery Publishing, Inc., 2004.

13. Herman, A. (2011, September). The Ultimate Stimulus. *The Weekly Standard*, 27-29.

14. Laffer, Arthur B., Moore, Stephen and Tanous, Peter J. The End of Prosperity: How Higher Taxes Will Doom the Economy. New York: Simon & Schuster, Inc., 2008.

15. Levin. Y. (2011, September). The Medicare Monster. *The Weekly Standard*, 22-27.

16. Montgomerie, Tim. (2011, August 24). Broken Britain. *Daily Telegraph*. Retrieved September 1, 2011 from http://www.telegraph.co.uk/

17. Medved, Michael. The 5 Big Lies About American Business: *Combating Smears Against The Free- Market Economy*. New York: Random House, Inc., 2009.

18. Paul Sweezy and Leo Huberman, "Introduction to Socialism," Monthly Review; available at: http://www.skeptically.org/socialism/id18.html [accessed March 20th, 2012].

19. Pipes, Sally C. The Truth about Obamacare: *What They Don't Want you to Know About Our New Health Care La*w. Washington D.C: Regnery Publishing, Inc., 2010.

20. Plimer, Ian. Heaven and Earth: *Global Warming the Missing Science*. Victoria Australia: Taylor Trade Publishing, 2009.

21. Singer, Fred S. and Avery, Dennis T. Unstoppable Global Warming: *Every 1500 Years*. Maryland: The Rowman & Littlefield Publishing Group, Inc., 2007.

22. Sowell, Thomas. Basic Economics: *A Common Sense Guide to the Economy*. New York: Basic Books, 2007.

23. Spencer, Robert. The Politically Incorrect Guide to Islam: *And the Crusades*. Regnery Publishing, Inc., 2005.

24. Steyn, Mark. America Alone: *The End of The World As We Know It*. Washington D.C: Regnery Publishing, Inc., 2006.

25. Thiessen, Marc A. Courting Disaster: *How the CIA Kept America Safe and How Barrack Obama is Inviting the Next Attack*. Washington D.C: Regnery Publishing, Inc., 2010.

26. Vogt, Claus and Leuschel, Roland. The Global Debt Trap: *How to Escape The Danger and Build A Fortune*. New Jersey: John Wiley and Sons, Inc., 2011.

27. Wright, Lawrence. The Looming Tower: *Al Queda and the Road to 9/11*. New York: Knopf Doubleday Publishing Group, 2006.

28. Williamson, Kevin D. The Politically Incorrect Guide to Socialism. Washington D.C: Regnery Publishing, Inc., 2011.